The Amazing Adventure

Discovering the New Me!

Bud Cox

Life Connection Publishing
Alpharetta, GA

Editor: Anne Alexander
Designer: Kim Smith
Illustrator: Mark James

Life Connection
Life Connection
12850 Highway 9 N
Suite 600 PMB 340
Alpharetta, GA 30004-4248

lifeconnection.com

facebook.com/theamazingadventure 

Life Connection leads children into a growing relationship with Jesus Christ by providing quality ministry resources that help children experience God's love. All of the proceeds from purchases of Life Connection Resources go toward providing ministry resources to children around the world.

Library of Congress Control Number: 2008909890

ISBN-13: 978-0-9717448-0-6
ISBN-10: 0-9717448-0-7

This book is dedicated to the Promised One - Jesus Christ.

"Before the mountains
were brought forth,
or ever you had formed
the earth and the world,
even from everlasting
to everlasting,
you are God."
Psalm 90:2

Preface

This book has been a work in progress from the time of my Bible College and Seminary years through my advanced training with Grace Ministries International to the current day. These experiences among many others have highlighted the journey of my own personal walk with Jesus Christ.

The Amazing Adventure, Discovering the New Me! originally started as single lessons that we mailed to our Life Connection Club members around the world. We started with the story of creation and continued through the Old and New Testaments, developing the common thread of God's love and acceptance and grace throughout the storyline. Life Connection has also recorded radio shows to complement the written lessons. With 31 lessons written, the next logical move was to compile them into a book.

I want to thank a team of volunteers and professionals who contributed to the shaping of this book from the early individual lessons to the finished product. Lisa O'Brien, Katy Pistole, and Anne Alexander all helped with editing the materials to get them to the "next level." Kim Smith has faithfully worked with me on the style and design since our first lessons in 2000. And Mark James made the characters of the Bible fun and real with his artistic flair.

I'm also grateful for the financial and prayer support Life Connection has received from hundreds of individuals and several churches since the ministry's inception in 1999. One anonymous donor gave year after year, which encouraged me to know that someone was watching out for the ministry, even though I didn't know who he or she was. It also helped to motivate me to communicate with all of our donors on a regular basis. Furthermore, I appreciate the great board of directors that oversees the vision and direction of the ministry. As various projects have emerged, they've encouraged me to walk through the open doors and trust God for the outcome.

And finally, my parents, Charlie and Ann Cox, have been some of my biggest "fans," along with my two sisters and their husbands—Hall and Becky (deceased) McKinley and Ron and Catherine Zampini. They have cheered me on by encouraging me to reach out to the many young people around the globe with the eternal message of God's love in Jesus Christ. My greatest inspiration for this project came from my nieces and nephews—Allison, David (and his wife Jenny), Hall, Paul (and his wife Katie), Caroline, and Elizabeth. As I have watched them blossom and grow through the years, I've seen the vast potential of the next generation to continue to spread God's message to those who haven't yet heard.

I trust this book will be used in your life and in countless lives of others in the years to come. Only eternity will tell the impact that a simple resource with a powerful message will have. Enjoy the journey of *The Amazing Adventure, Discovering the New Me!*

Episodes

Foreward

What do you want to do when you grow up?

Who do you want to be?

What makes you feel really happy?

Where would you like to go?

Are you ready to go on an adventure?

Remember the adventures of Swiss Family Robinson? Wow, what an unforgettable journey—shipwrecked on an island where turtle rides replace bicycles and your bedroom is in a tree house, a place where pirates are real and family fun is on the beach of your own island!

The Amazing Adventure, Discovering the New Me! will take you on a journey to your own island—to the place where your heart lives. You'll discover the truth about a genuine friend who will always be with you, an authentic hero who will rescue you from the bad guys and introduce you to the good guys. You'll find out how this new friend has fought battles for other people and rescued them as well.

Bud Cox, the author, is your friend. He's been to these kinds of places and remembers well the adventure he found there. Through this book, he'll take you to the same exciting places. You won't forget what happens on this amazing adventure.

Foreward by Tom Grady
Operation Freedom, Inc., a non-profit ministry

Episode 1

The Adventure Begins: Ultimate Friendship

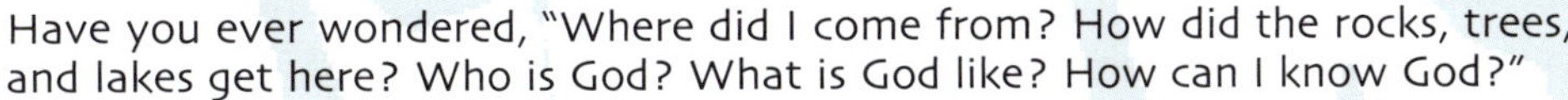

Have you ever wondered, "Where did I come from? How did the rocks, trees, and lakes get here? Who is God? What is God like? How can I know God?"

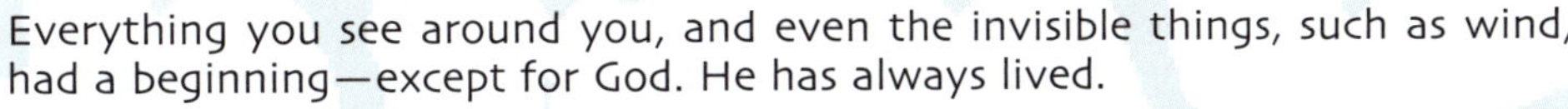

Everything you see around you, and even the invisible things, such as wind, had a beginning—except for God. He has always lived.

God lived before anything, anyone, or even time itself existed. He lives forever, and He will never die. He is like a flame that stays lit all the time and never burns out. Seeing His glory is like opening a huge curtain in a dark room and letting the sunshine in. The light makes everything in the room so much easier to see.

Now, use your imagination, as we journey to the beginning of time to look at the story, "The Adventure Begins: Ultimate Friendship."

Story

(Story adapted from Genesis 1:1 to 2:3)

This is God's story. He is telling the story as if He is talking to you.

In the beginning, I created the sky and the earth. I spoke, and all creation came into being, out of nothing. The earth was formless, and darkness covered the ocean. I created light and separated the light from the darkness on the first day.

On the second day, I created the air, which had water above and below it. The water above the air was like a mist in the sky. The water below the air was the ocean.

On the third day, I spoke, and the water below the air gathered so that dry land would appear. I called the land "earth" and the water "seas." I enabled the earth to grow plants, and the plants produced fruits and grains, similar to what you now eat. The plants also produced seeds for making new plants. At this point, I was still getting things ready for My special creation, YOU.

On the fourth day, I created the sun, the moon, and the stars to separate day and night. I put the earth on an axis, like a spinning top, and sent it orbiting around the sun to make the seasons, days, and years. I made the larger light, the sun, to brighten the day. I made the smaller light, the moon, to illuminate the night. Have you been outside lately on a clear night? I created the dazzling canopy of stars that hang over you. I spoke all of this into being with a gigantic sound. The sound echoed out over the vast creation. Can you imagine the planets trying to maintain their orbits without My direction? Without My design, the universe would be in total chaos.

On the fifth day, I created everything that lives in the water, including fish, eels, and crabs. I created the birds that fly overhead. I gave the fish and birds their many different colors, shapes, and sizes, and I know everything about each of them. I also made them able to reproduce.

On the sixth day, I filled the earth with animals, reptiles, insects, and other land creatures. Some of them were so small that they seemed invisible. Others were huge. All of them reproduced more of their own kind. I called all of My creation good.

Yet, none of these creatures could have a friendship with Me. So I created man and woman in My image and likeness. This means they could think, feel, choose, and imagine. No other creature was like them. The first man and woman had My life in them. I created them to be My friends. I blessed them and said, "Have a lot of children." I let them take care of everything on the earth. Do you know what this means? It means that YOU, above everything else that I have created, are very special to Me. You are My most precious creation.

By the seventh day, I had completed all of My work of creation, so I rested. All that I had created was very good. I had made a beautiful, pure world full of life. As you can see, all of this could not have come into being without Me. I give life, and I preserve life. I want you to know Me as your Life Giver.

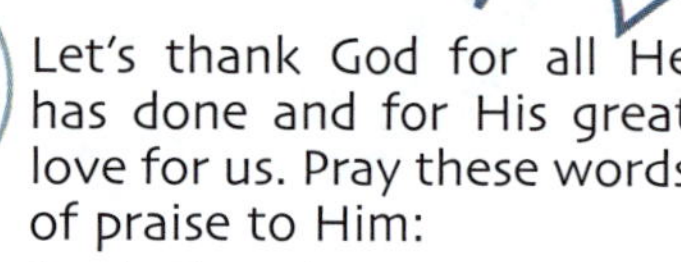

Let's thank God for all He has done and for His great love for us. Pray these words of praise to Him:

God, thank You that You created the sky and the earth; You spoke all creation into being, out of nothing. You created man and woman in Your image and likeness, to be Your friends. You created me to think, feel, choose, and imagine. Thank You that I am special to You—that I am Your most precious creation. I want to know You as my Life Giver.

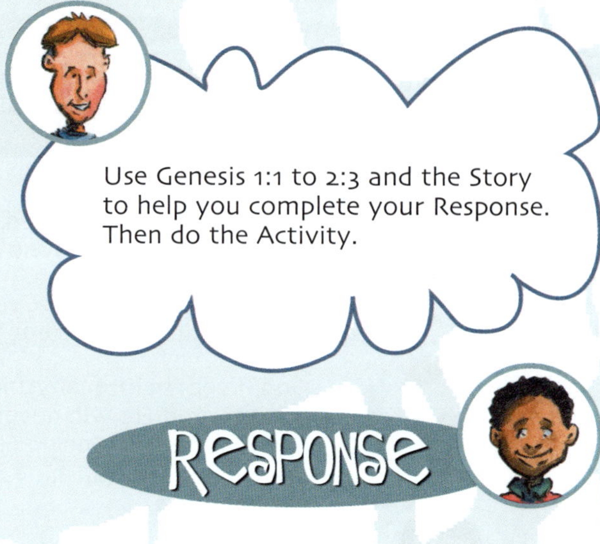

RESPONSE

1. God spoke, and all creation came into being, out of nothing.

❑ True ❑ False

2. God created ______________________________ in His image and likeness.
a. man and woman
b. animals
c. plants

3. The first man and woman had God's __________ in them.

4. What is another name for God in this story?

____

5. You are special to God, and you are His most precious creation. How can knowing this improve your family life, friendships, and activities? ______________________________

____

____

____

6. Read this verse: "Then God saw everything that He had made, and indeed it was very good" (Genesis 1:31).

Now write a letter to God or draw a picture about what you like about His creation and why. Thank Him for those things.

Creation Jumble

Oh no! The order of creation below is all mixed up. Use Genesis 1:1 to 2:3 and the Story to write the correct order in the boxes. Number each box to show when the events took place in the creation story.

- [ ] Gathered water so that land appeared; enabled earth to grow plants
- [ ] Created everything that lives in the water (e.g., fish, eels, and crabs); created birds
- [ ] Created animals, reptiles, insects, other land creatures, and man
- [ ] Created light; separated light from darkness
- [ ] Rested
- [ ] Created sun, moon, and stars to separate day and night
- [ ] Created air; divided water above and below the air

What might have happened if God had created the world in this mixed-up order? (For example, man would have frozen to death if God had created him before creating the sun.) ____________
____
____

What did you learn about God's character from the Activity? ____________
____
____

Let's praise God right now for being in control of the order of creation.

Episode 2

Adam: Hiding From Love

Would you like to have been the first person to live on the earth? What would it have been like to live in a beautiful place, walk and talk with God every day, and have all of your favorite foods?

That's how it was for Adam and his wife, Eve. They lived in a beautiful place called the Garden of Eden. They had perfect friendship with God and with each other, and they had wonderful food to eat.

Adam and his wife were the first people to live on the earth. They had everything they needed, but they lost it all.

Now, use your imagination, as we journey back through time to look at the story, "Adam: Hiding from Love."

(Story adapted from Genesis 2:4 to 3:24)

My name is Adam. I am excited to share with you how God worked in my life.

God, the Creator of all things, thought of me before the world was made. I was part of His forever plan. God created my body from the dust of the ground. I began living when He put His life in me. I could see, hear, smell, taste, and touch. I could think, feel, choose, and imagine. God created me to be His friend. Isn't He amazing?

God placed me in the Garden of Eden. The Garden of Eden had many trees. The Garden also had two special trees: the tree of life and the tree of knowing good and evil. I would live forever if I ate fruit from the tree of life. But I would die if I ate fruit from the tree of knowing good and evil. That meant my body would die one day, and I would lose my perfect friendship with God. God didn't want me to eat fruit from that tree. God loved me. He let me choose whether to depend upon Him or depend upon myself.

God saw that it was not good for me to be alone. I had named all the animals God created, but none of them was like me. None could be my close friend. So God put me into a deep sleep and took a rib from my body. He used the rib to make a woman. When God brought the woman to me, I knew we were made for each other. She became my wife. I named her Eve.

One day, a serpent came to Eve. The serpent was actually Satan, an enemy of God. The serpent asked Eve whether God had really said that we must not eat fruit from any tree in the Garden. Eve said that if she and I ate fruit from the tree of knowing good and evil, we would die. The serpent said that we would not die. But that was a lie. The serpent also said that we would know good and evil, just like God does.

The tree of knowing good and evil looked beautiful to Eve. Maybe she thought, "I want to taste good things. I want to be as wise as God is." Eve ate the fruit and then gave some to me. I ate it, too. Right away, we knew we had made a big mistake. Eating the fruit made us ashamed and afraid. We realized we weren't wearing any clothes, so we covered ourselves with fig leaves.

Late in the day, we heard God walking in the Garden. We tried to hide, but He knew where we were. He knew everything about us, and He still loved us! He also knew we would choose to depend upon ourselves instead of upon Him. This is what "to sin" means. He wanted us to admit our sin to Him. We were afraid, so we made excuses. I blamed Eve for giving the fruit to me. Then Eve blamed the serpent for tricking her.

God said everything had changed. Women would feel pain during childbirth. We would have to work hard to grow food. Our bodies would die in time and become dust again. The worst of it was that all people would be born with sin in their lives. Sin meant death for all people. Sin made a gap between all people and God. Yet, God promised to make a bridge over the gap.

God made clothes out of animal skins and put them on Eve and me. Then He sent us out of the Garden. He placed angels and a flaming sword near the tree of life. He wanted to protect us from eating its fruit and living forever. Why? We had sin in us. God did not want us to have sin in us forever! He always loved us.

Let's thank God that He always loves us. Pray these words of praise to Him:

God, You thought of me before the world was made. Even when I try to hide, You know where I am. You know everything about me. Thank You for always loving me.

Response

1. Why did the serpent lie to Eve? Hint: Who wanted good things for Adam and Eve (God or the serpent)?

____

____

2. What happened after Adam and Eve ate the fruit?

____

3. Why can't we hide from God? ____________

____

____

4. "To sin" means ______________________________

____.

a. to depend upon ourselves instead of upon God
b. to wear fig leaves
c. to wear animal skins

5. All people are born with sin in their lives. Sin meant death for all people. Sin made a gap between all people and God.

❑ True ❑ False

6. Why did God send Adam and Eve out of the Garden of Eden (see Genesis 3:22–23)? ________

____

____

7. God placed angels and a flaming sword to guard the tree of life. What does that tell you about God?
a. God is mean. He did not want Adam and Eve to enjoy good food.
b. God is unforgiving. He wanted Adam and Eve to always feel ashamed.
c. God is loving. He did not want Adam and Eve to have sin in them forever.

8. God knows everything about us. He ______
____.

a. punishes us
b. hides from us
c. loves us

9. Read this verse: "And they heard . . . God walking in the garden in the cool of the day, and Adam and his wife hid themselves from the presence of . . . God" (Genesis 3:8).

Now write a letter to God or draw a picture about a time you hid because you felt ashamed. Then thank God for knowing everything about you. Thank Him for loving you.

Young Children: Draw a picture of Adam and Eve hiding from God.

In The Garden

Find and circle the following words hidden in the puzzle below. The words may be forward, backward, horizontal, vertical, or diagonal.

ADAM	GOD	SIN
EVE	LOVE	TREE
GARDEN	SERPENT	

```
T E V O L X G J X B W K N I S
E N A X Y B I F O P V V E Q T
E H E V U R L X I C I Z V C D
M W Q P X G U N N P D O E L A
R M I V R A O Y K D A S D G A
S E D N C E V I X K V V G D N
D B D D P X S E E R T Y A G I
Q O F F L R F B N W S Q R A Y
G N A Z G R L J P M U E D D N
X N K W S O D I R Z J Q E A Z
K D O B C T U H Y O F M N M A
Q O E A U A I G B H J W G W I
```

Episode 3

Noah: Promise Made

What would you do if it rained for forty days and forty nights? How would you feel if you couldn't go outside for over a year because your yard was flooded?

That's how it was for Noah, a man who lived many years ago. He and his family stayed inside a huge boat for more than a year during a rainstorm and flood. The water covered the entire earth, and it destroyed everything. Nothing like this had ever happened.

Noah, his wife, and his three sons and their wives escaped death from the great flood. They trusted in God, and He saved them.

Now, use your imagination, as we journey back through time to look at the story, "Noah: Promise Made."

Story

(Story adapted from Genesis 6:5 to 9:29)

My name is Noah. I am excited to share with you how God worked in my life.

People lived a long time during my day. After I was 500 years old, my wife and I had three sons, named Shem, Ham, and Japheth. They grew up and had wives, too.

People on the earth were wicked. They didn't believe in God. They would not trust in Him. They had "sin" in them. God felt pain in His heart because sin meant death for all people. Sin made a gap between all people and God. God decided to destroy people, animals, birds, and crawling things by a flood. But I trusted in God. He accepted me. God called me blameless. Nothing could separate me from His love. God saved my family and me, and we depended upon Him. He also kept a few of each kind of animal, bird, and crawling thing, so they could keep living after the flood.

God had a "forever plan." As part of that plan, God said to build a huge wooden boat, called an "ark." God said the ark would be 450 feet long, 75 feet wide, and 45 feet high. It was as long as one and one-half football fields! The ark had three decks, with rooms for my family and the animals, birds, and crawling things. The ark had only one door, though. The door was God's "One Way" to be saved from the flood.

The animals, birds, and crawling things came to me in pairs. They went into the ark. Then my family and I went into the ark. We all entered through the "One Door." Then God closed the door to the ark.

After a week, the underground springs broke open, and the clouds poured out rain. It rained for forty days and forty nights. The water lifted the ark off the ground. The ark floated above the highest mountains. Everything on the earth died, except us in the ark. The animals kept us busy day and night. We fed them, cleaned up after them, and helped care for their babies. We were in God's floating zoo!

God did not forget about us in the ark. After the rain stopped, God sent a strong wind over the earth to make the water go down. The ark finally came to rest on a mountain. But we had to stay in the ark for several more months because the water was still too high.

Finally, we left the ark. It had been our home for more than a year. When we stepped onto dry land, we worshiped God. We were amazed that He would save us, out of all the people on the earth. God promised to never again destroy all living things by a flood. He placed a beautiful rainbow high in the clouds to remind us of this promise. The next time you see a rainbow, remember that God keeps all of His promises.

After the flood, we sometimes forgot that God keeps His promises. We did not always depend upon Him, but He always loved us and accepted us. Nothing could break our friendship with Him. God wants you to have friendship with Him and to be safe and secure in His "ark of life."

Let's thank God for His forever plan and for His great love for us. Pray these words of praise to Him:

God, thank You for promising to never again destroy all living things by a flood. Thank You for keeping all of Your promises and for always loving me. I want to have friendship with You and to be safe and secure in Your "ark of life."

Use Genesis 6:5 to 9:29 and the Story to help you complete your Response. Then do the Activity.

RESPONSE

1. People on the earth were wicked. They would not trust in God. They had "sin" in them. Which sentence describes God's feelings about sin?
a. God felt pain in His heart because sin meant death for all people.
b. God hated people because of sin.

2. Sin made a gap between all people and God.
❑ True ❑ False

3. God decided to destroy people, animals, birds, and crawling things by a flood. God said to build an ark! How did Noah respond to God? Which sentence below is true?
a. Noah did not depend upon God. He built the ark after the rain started falling.
b. Noah depended upon God. He built the ark before the rain started falling.
c. Noah complained to God. Noah didn't want his neighbors to laugh at him!

4. After the flood, God promised to never again destroy all living things by a flood. He placed a beautiful rainbow high in the clouds to remind us of this promise. What does the rainbow tell us about God?
a. God keeps His promises on rainy days only.
b. God has a bad memory. The rainbow helps Him remember His promises.
c. God always keeps His promises.

5. Read these verses: "Then God spoke to Noah and to his sons with him, saying: . . . Thus I establish My covenant with you: Never again shall all flesh be cut off by the waters of the flood; never again shall there be a flood to destroy the earth" (Genesis 9:8, 11).

Now write a letter to God or draw a picture about a time someone broke a promise to you. Describe or show how you felt. Then write or draw about a time you broke a promise. Describe or show how you felt. Thank God that He always keeps His promises.

Young Children: Draw a picture of Noah, his family, and the animals on the ark.

Promise in a Rainbow

God promised never to destroy all living things again by a flood. He placed a beautiful rainbow high in the clouds to remind us of this promise.

1. Read the promises below, and write one on each rainbow. Use a pen. Then color the rainbows lightly. The next time you feel disappointed, look at these rainbows. They will remind you of God's wonderful promises to you.

- God does not forget about you.
- God always loves you.
- God keeps all of His promises.

2. Do you have a friend who needs to know God's promises? You can make more rainbows and write God's promises on them. Then give the rainbows to your friend.

Episode 4

Abraham: Promise Kept

Has anyone ever promised you something so big that you wondered how it could happen? Did you let yourself hope for it? Did you trust the person to keep the promise? Did you try to make it happen on your own?

Abraham lived many years ago. He and his wife were unable to have children. However, God promised them a son. God also promised them several other wonderful things. Abraham must have wondered how God's promises could happen.

Now, use your imagination, as we journey back through time to look at the story, "Abraham: Promise Kept."

Story

(Story adapted from Genesis 12:1–9, 13:14–18, 15:1 to 18:15, 21:1–21)

My name is Abraham. I am excited to share with you how God worked in my life.

When I was seventy-five years old, I left my home and went to the land of Canaan. I took my wife Sarah, my nephew Lot, and everything we owned. I was an older man. My wife and I had no children. Yet, God said He would make a great nation out of my family. God also said that people in the future would know about me. He said I would be a blessing to all people on the earth. I didn't understand.

We finally arrived in the land of Canaan. God told me to look north, south, east, and west. He promised to give my family all the land I saw. He also said He would give me many descendants. They would be as many as the stars in the sky. Do you know how many people that is? It was impossible for me to count the stars, but I believed God. God accepted me, and I trusted in Him.

During the next several years, God reminded me of His promise. He did not want me to lose hope. God had promised a huge family for Sarah and me, but we still had no children—and I was about eighty-five years old! So Sarah suggested that I have a child with her slave girl, Hagar. I listened to Sarah. Hagar and I had a son. I named him Ishmael. God said that Ishmael would become a great nation, too.

Thirteen years later, God reminded me again that He would give Sarah and me a son. I laughed and said to myself, "Could I have a child when I'm one hundred years older and Sarah is ninety years old?"

I asked God to keep His promise through Ishmael. But God said, "No, Sarah will have a son named Isaac."

When Sarah heard that she would have a son in her old age, she laughed to herself. Normally, it is impossible for older women to have babies. Yet, God assured me that nothing was too hard for Him.

God kept His promise, and our son Isaac was born. The name "Isaac" means "laughter." Sarah laughed with joy that God gave us a son in our old age! She said that everyone who heard about this would laugh with her.

Sarah wanted to throw Hagar and Ishmael out of our house. She wanted Isaac to inherit everything we had. She didn't want Ishmael to inherit any of our things. This troubled me very much because Ishmael was my son, too. But God said not to be troubled. His promise would come through the descendants of Isaac. He would also make the descendants of Ishmael into a great nation. He would do this because Ishmael was my son, too.

So, I gave food and water to Hagar and sent her away. She carried these things along with her son. She wandered in the desert. When all the water was gone, Hagar thought her son would die, so she began to cry. God heard Hagar crying and an angel asked her what was wrong. The angel said not to be afraid but to help the boy up because God would make his descendants into a great nation. Then, God showed Hagar a well of water. She filled her bag and gave the boy a drink. God was with Ishmael as he grew up. He lived in the desert, and he married a woman from Egypt.

I didn't always depend upon God, but He never forgot His promise. He blessed me and made me a blessing to others.

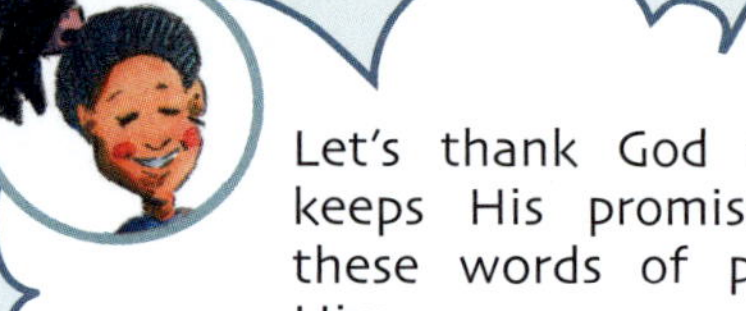

Let's thank God that He keeps His promises. Pray these words of praise to Him:

God, You assure me that nothing is too hard for You. Thank You that You keep Your promises. You always take care of Your people.

Use Genesis 12:1–9, 13:14–18, 15:1 to 18:15, 21:1–21 and the Story to help you complete your Response. Then do the Activity.

Response

1. God said He would give Abraham many descendants. They would be as many as the stars in the sky.

❑ True ❑ False

2. Sarah suggested that Abraham have a child with Sarah's slave girl, Hagar.
a. Abraham listened to Sarah, and Ishmael was born.
b. Abraham said no to Sarah. He waited for God to keep His promise.
c. Abraham listened to Sarah, but nothing happened.

3. God reminded Abraham that He would give Sarah a son. Abraham __________________ and said to himself, "Could I have a child when I'm one hundred years old and Sarah is ninety years old?"
a. smiled
b. cried
c. laughed

4. God kept His ____________________ and Isaac was born.

5. Read this verse: "Is anything too hard for the LORD? At the appointed time I will return to you, according to the time of life [in one year], and Sarah shall have a son" (Genesis 18:14).

Now write a letter to God or draw a picture about a time something good happened that seemed impossible. Thank God that nothing is too hard for Him.

Young Children: Draw a picture of Abraham and Sarah in their old age.

God Keeps His Promises

God said that Sarah would have a son in her old age. He also said that Abraham's descendants would be as many as the stars in the sky. Can you count the stars? Can anyone? God can. Nothing is too hard for Him. Abraham had to travel a long way and wait many years for God's promise to be fulfilled. God reminded Abraham of the promise several times, so Abraham would not lose hope. God always keeps His promises.

The puzzle below contains a message about God's promises. To uncover the message, find the first letter next to the arrow, and skip every other letter. You will make two trips around the circle. Write the message on the blanks inside the circle. Then respond by circling "YES" or "NO."

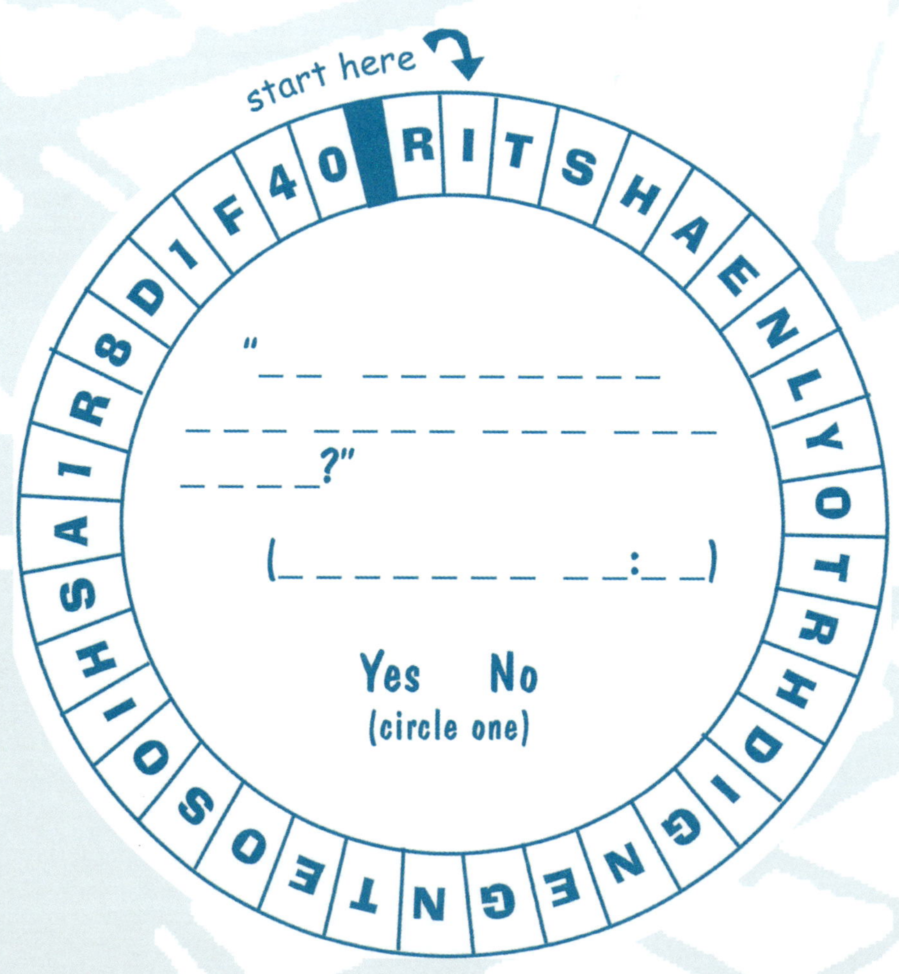

Episode 5

Abraham: All About Faith

What if someone gave you a wonderful gift, promised you more gifts, and then asked you to give them up?

God kept His promise to Abraham and Sarah. In their old age, Isaac was born—just like God had promised. God also promised to give Abraham several other wonderful things. But then God made a hard request that didn't make any sense to Abraham. He asked Abraham to give them all up.

Now, use your imagination, as we journey back through time to look at the story, "Abraham: All About Faith."

Story

(Story adapted from Genesis 22:1–18)

My name is Abraham. I am excited to share with you how God worked in my life.

During the next several years, God reminded me of His promise that He would give us a son. He did not want me to lose hope. But after twenty-five years, my wife and I still didn't have any children! Yet, God assured me that nothing was too hard for Him. God did keep His promise, and Isaac was born when I was one hundred years old and Sarah was ninety. God always keeps His promises—even when they seem impossible.

Isaac was our pride and joy. We had waited so long for him to join our family. He grew up to be a fine teenager, and one day, God said to me, "Take Isaac to the mountain and sacrifice him." I loved Isaac more than my own life, but God wanted me to kill him and burn him on an altar. God had promised that my descendants would be as many as the stars in the sky. He had promised to make me a blessing to all people on the earth. How could God keep His promises if my son died? I didn't understand, but I knew God could be trusted, even when I didn't understand why He was asking me to do this.

I depended upon God, and early the next morning, I saddled my donkey. Two of my servants, my son Isaac, and I set out for the mountain. Then, on the third day, we approached the place of sacrifice. I told my servants to wait with the donkey while Isaac and I went up to worship. Isaac didn't know that God wanted me to sacrifice him. He carried the wood on his back, and I carried the fire and the knife.

As we walked, Isaac said, "Father, we have fire and wood, but where is the lamb for the sacrifice?"

I answered, "God will provide the lamb, my son."

Finally, we came to the place of sacrifice. I built an altar and arranged the wood on it. Then I tied up my son Isaac and laid him on the wood. I took the knife and prepared to kill him. Yet Isaac didn't say anything or try to run away. Isaac knew he could trust me because I depended upon God.

Just then, the angel of the Lord called to me from heaven, "Abraham!"

"Here I am," I said.

"Do not harm the boy. I know now that you depend upon Me. You have not kept back your only son from Me."

A male sheep was caught in the bushes. I killed it and sacrificed it on the altar. My son was saved because God provided a lamb. I named that place "God provides."

Then the angel of the Lord called to me a second time. He said, "You have not kept back your only son from Me. I promise by My name to give you many descendants. They will be as many as the stars in the sky and the sand on the seashore. Through your family, all people on earth will be blessed."

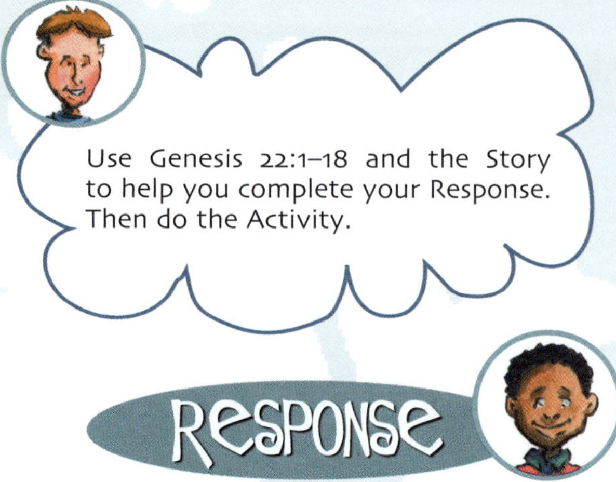

Response

1. Isaac was Abraham and Sarah's surprise.

❑ True ❑ False

2. Abraham loved Isaac more than his own life, but God wanted Abraham to kill Isaac and burn him on an altar. How could God keep His promises if Isaac died? Abraham didn't understand, but he ______________________

______________________________________.

a. knew God would save Isaac somehow
b. knew God could be trusted

3. Abraham and Isaac approached the place of sacrifice. Isaac carried the wood on his back, and Abraham carried the fire and the knife. As they walked, Isaac said, "Father, we have fire and wood, but where is the lamb for the sacrifice?" Abraham answered, ______________________

____

a. "You are the sacrifice."
b. "I don't know."
c. "God will provide the lamb, my son."

4. At the place of sacrifice, Abraham built an altar, arranged the wood on it, tied up his son, and laid him on the wood. Then he took the knife and prepared to kill him. Yet Isaac didn't say anything or try to run away. Why not?
a. Isaac knew he could trust his father because his father depended upon God.
b. Isaac knew that his father wouldn't really kill him.
c. Abraham had blindfolded Isaac and knocked him out.

5. The angel of the Lord said, "Do not harm the boy. I know now that you depend upon Me. You have not kept back your only son from Me." Abraham saw a male sheep caught in the bushes. He killed it and sacrificed it on the altar. Isaac was saved because God provided a lamb. Why didn't God tell Abraham that He planned all along to save Isaac?
a. God wanted to play a mean trick on Abraham.
b. God wanted to surprise Abraham.
c. God wanted Abraham to depend upon Him.

6. Read this verse: "And Abraham said, 'My son, God will provide for Himself the lamb for a burnt offering.' So the two of them went together" (Genesis 22:8).

Now write a letter to God or draw a picture about a time you had to do something impossible and someone did it in your place. Thank God that He always provides for us.

Young Children: Draw a picture of Abraham and Isaac at the altar.

GOD WILL PROVIDE

Directions: Start at the arrow, and follow the letters until you reach the period.

I	W	D	O	G	N	O	S
L	A						Y
L	P	B					M
F	O	R	R				D
F	T		O	A			I
E	N			V	H		A
R	R		F	B	I	A	S
I	U		O	M		D	M
N	B		R	A			E
G	.	A		L	E	H	T

Write the verse on the lines below. How does this story give you confidence that God will provide for you too?

________ ________, "____ ______, ______ ________ ____________ ______

________ ______ __ _________ _________."

Episode 6

Jacob: From Deceit to Brokenness

Have you ever acted deceptively or selfishly? Have you ever grabbed for something, thinking that this behavior would work to your advantage, only to discover that more harm was caused? How did you react to this discovery?

Jacob acted deceptively and selfishly. He was always looking out for himself, trying to get everything to work to his advantage. But he later discovered that greater harm was caused because of his behavior.

Now, use your imagination, as we journey back through time to look at the story, "Jacob: From Deceit to Brokenness."

Story

(Story adapted from Genesis 25:19–34, 27:1 to 33:20, 35:1–29)

My name is Jacob. I am excited to share with you how God worked in my life.

When I was born, I came out of my mother's womb grabbing my brother Esau's heel. My brother grew up to become a skilled hunter, but I liked to stay at home. I was cooking stew one day when Esau came in from hunting. He asked me for some stew, and I told him that first he would have to sell me his rights as the firstborn son. Esau was so hungry he agreed, so I gave him some stew.

Our father, Isaac, was blind and didn't know how much longer he had to live. He wanted to give Esau, the firstborn, a special blessing before he died, so he asked Esau to kill an animal for us to eat as part of the ceremony. After Esau left, my mother, Rebekah, quickly prepared two goats just as my father liked them. She told me to take the food into him because she wanted me to get the blessing instead of Esau. She even put animal skins on my arms because Esau was hairy. I took the food to my father, acting like I was Esau. He asked how I killed the animal so quickly. He also was suspicious because he recognized my voice, but because I felt hairy like Esau, my father ate, drank, and blessed me. Just after I left, Esau came in with the animal he had killed. Esau was so

angry, he thought about killing me, so my father sent me away to where my mother's brother lived. His name was Laban. On the way, I fell asleep. I dreamed that there was a ladder from the earth that reached into heaven. I saw the angels of God going up and coming down the ladder, and the Lord was standing above the ladder. He gave me the same promise that He gave to Abraham and to my father, Isaac. When I awoke, I was afraid, so I made a promise to God because I wanted Him to protect and provide for me.

Later, I met Rachel, Uncle Laban's youngest daughter, and I fell in love with her. I told Uncle Laban that I would work seven years for him if I could marry Rachel. He agreed, but after the seven years, Uncle Laban tricked me into marrying his older daughter, Leah. He said I could marry Rachel after seven more years of work. I loved her enough to work seven more years, and then I married Rachel. There was much jealousy between the sisters because I loved Rachel more than Leah.

On the way back to my homeland, I sent a message to Esau that I wanted to see him. The messenger returned saying that Esau was coming to meet me with 400 men. Instead of trusting God, I was afraid that Esau would kill us. I prepared a gift of several herds of animals for Esau, hoping that he would accept me and forgive me.

That night a Man came and wrestled with me until morning. I was so determined not to lose that He put my hip out of joint. When the Man told me to let go of Him, I said only if He blessed me. The Man changed my name from Jacob to Israel. I had seen God "face to face," but my life was spared.

When Esau and I met, I bowed down in submission to him, and he ran to meet me. It was a good reunion, and then we went our separate ways. As you can see, I thought I could deceive people and fix my problems, but more trouble always came. I constantly tried to manipulate circumstances, people, and even God. In spite of this, God still worked in my life, and He used these difficult circumstances to carry on His family line to the Promised One. God demonstrates His love and grace as He works through our lives—even when we rebel—we can't change His plans.

Let's thank God that He always is working in our lives. Pray these words of praise to Him:

God, thank You that I can trust You. I don't have to be afraid or try to manipulate You. When I try to fix my problems by deceiving people, more trouble comes. But even if I rebel, You still work in my life. You use difficult circumstances to carry on Your family line to the Promised One. Thank You that You demonstrate Your love and grace in my life.

Use Genesis 25:19–34, 27:1 to 33:20, 35:1–29 and the Story to help you complete your Response. Then do the Activity.

1. When Jacob was born, he came out of his mother's womb grabbing his brother Esau's heel.

❑ True ❑ False

2. Esau asked Jacob for some ______________, and Jacob told him that first he would have to sell him his rights as the firstborn son.
a. animal skins
b. stew
c. help in hunting

3. Rebekah told Jacob to take the food into Isaac because she wanted ________________ to get the blessing instead of ____________________.

4. Uncle Laban agreed, but after the seven years, he ____________________ Jacob into marrying his older daughter, Leah.

5. Instead of ___________________ God, Jacob was _____________________ that Esau would kill them.

6. Jacob thought he could ________________ people and fix his problems, but more __________ always came.

7. Read this verse: "I have seen thy face as though I had seen the face of God" (Genesis 33:10).

Now write a letter to God or draw a picture about a time you deceived (tricked) someone or about a time when you felt deceived by someone else. Think about what you learned from that experience. Did you see God's grace at work in the situation?

Young Children: Draw a picture of Jacob wrestling with the Man.

Favorites

Isaac (the dad) loved Esau (the oldest) more than Jacob. And Rebekah (the mom) loved Jacob (the youngest) more than Esau. God doesn't intend for parents to have "favorite" children in a family, but when it happens, there are a lot of hurt feelings. Unscramble the following words to discover how Esau and Jacob might have felt.

OESLUAJ ______________

THAE ______________

GENAR ______________

TRETIB ______________

LITUG ______________

HMEAS ______________

Episode 7

Joseph: Bigger Than Our Troubles

Have you ever known something was about to happen, but no one believed you? How did you feel? How did people treat you?

Joseph had two dreams that he thought would come true, but his brothers didn't believe him. In fact, the dreams made Joseph's brothers so mad that they began to hate Joseph and look for a way to get rid of him.

Now, use your imagination, as we journey back through time to look at the story, "Joseph: Bigger Than Our Troubles."

Story

(Story adapted from Genesis 37, 39 to 41)

My name is Joseph. I am excited to share with you how God worked in my life.

I grew up in a big family. I had ten older brothers, one older sister, and one younger brother. My father, Jacob, loved me more than he loved my brothers and sister. When I was seventeen, my father made a colorful robe for me. My brothers hated me for being my father's favorite son. They could not say a kind word to me. Twice, I had dreams that my family would bow down to me. I told my family about the dreams, and my brothers hated me more than ever.

Sometimes my father sent me to check on my brothers. One of those times, my brothers saw me coming and plotted to kill me! But two of my brothers convinced them not to kill me. Instead, my brothers threw me into a dry well. Then they sold me to some traders traveling to Egypt.

Later, my brothers killed a goat and dipped my colorful robe into the blood. They brought the bloodstained robe to my father and told my father that they had "found" it. My father thought a wild animal had torn me to pieces and eaten me. My father mourned for months. My brothers tried to comfort him, but they would not tell him the truth.

Meanwhile, I went to Egypt. A man named Potiphar bought me as his slave. Potiphar was captain of the guard and an officer for Pharaoh, the king of Egypt. I began serving in Potiphar's house. God was with me and gave me success in everything I did. So Potiphar put me in charge of his house and everything he owned. He trusted me with everything he had.

Potiphar's wife wanted me to lie down with her, but I told her no. Potiphar trusted me. I could not lie down with his wife. It was a sin against God. I tried to avoid Potiphar's wife, but she would not leave me alone. One day, she grabbed my coat as I walked by. She asked me again to lie down with her. I ran out of the house, without my coat. She accused me of mistreating her. I hadn't touched her! I was Potiphar's favorite servant, but he believed his wife. He became very angry and put me into prison.

God showed kindness to me while I was in prison. The prison warden put me in charge of the prisoners. He trusted me because God was with me. God gave me success in everything I did.

In prison, I met Pharaoh's wine server and his baker. They each had dreams with special meanings. I told them that only God can explain the meanings of dreams. Then I asked them to tell me the dreams. The dreams showed that the wine server would return to his work, but the baker would be hanged. I asked the wine server to remember me and tell Pharaoh about me, so I could get out of prison. Three days later, both servants were released from prison. The wine server went back to serving wine, but the baker was hanged, just like the dreams showed. However, the wine server forgot to tell Pharaoh about me. So I stayed in prison.

Two years later, Pharaoh had two dreams that troubled him. Pharaoh's wine server remembered me and told Pharaoh about me. Pharaoh called for me and brought me out of prison. He told me that he'd had two dreams that no one could explain. I told him that I could not explain the meaning of dreams. God would do it. The dreams showed that God would bring seven years of plenty and seven years of hunger. During the first seven years, there would be plenty of food, but during the next seven years, people would forget what it was like to have plenty of food. The hunger would be severe.

I suggested that Pharaoh put someone in charge of Egypt. I also suggested that Pharaoh choose officers. They would gather and store food during the seven years of plenty. This food would be used during the seven years of hunger, so the people wouldn't die. Pharaoh liked my idea, so he put me in charge of Egypt! I had been a prisoner. Suddenly, I was the second-highest official in Egypt!

In all my troubles, God cared for me. He gave me success in everything I did. I didn't blame Him for my troubles; I depended upon Him. I couldn't do anything on my own, but God planned to save many people through me. People meant to hurt me, but God carried out His plan.

1. Jacob made a colorful robe for Joseph. Joseph's brothers hated him for being the favorite son.

❑ True ❑ False

2. What did Joseph's brothers do to him?

____

3. Joseph became a slave in Potiphar's house. But God gave Joseph success in everything he did. Potiphar put Joseph in charge of __________

____.

4. Potiphar's wife lied about Joseph, and Potiphar believed her. Joseph went to prison. But God gave Joseph success in everything he did. The prison warden put Joseph in charge of _________

__________________________________.

5. Joseph told Pharaoh's wine server and his baker what the dreams meant. The wine server forgot about Joseph, so Joseph stayed in prison for two years. Then Pharaoh had two dreams. The wine server remembered Joseph. God gave Joseph success in everything he did. Joseph told Pharaoh what the dreams meant. Pharaoh put Joseph in charge of __________________________________.

6. Joseph did not blame God for his troubles—he depended upon God through them. How might the story have been different if Joseph had depended upon himself instead of upon God?

____

____

How might you have responded if you had been sold, put in prison, and forgotten? ___________

____

____

7. Read this verse: "So Joseph answered Pharaoh, saying, 'It is not in me; God will give Pharaoh an answer of peace'" (Genesis 41:16).

Now write a letter to God or draw a picture about a time that something happened that only God could do. (For example, your grandmother recovered from cancer; your dog came home after being lost; or your dad lost his job, and your parents received an envelope full of cash—in the mail.)

Young Children: Draw a picture about Joseph's life in Egypt.

Troubles

Troubles happen because there is sin in the world. Joseph did not blame God for his troubles. Instead, he depended upon God. God made Joseph successful in the middle of troubles. Joseph's troubles were out of his control. Many times, our troubles are out of our control too, but we can learn from Joseph how to respond.

List your troubles below:

1. ______________________________

2. ______________________________

3. ______________________________

4. ______________________________

5. ______________________________

Are any of your troubles bigger than God is? Praise God that He is bigger than our troubles. Praise Him that He is in control and nothing is too hard for Him.

Episode 8

Joseph: Something Good

When people hurt you, do you feel mad, sad, afraid, or disappointed? Do you blame yourself or others? Do you blame God? Do you look for the good things in the situation? Do you believe that God can make good things come out of a bad situation?

Joseph's brothers tried to get rid of him. They sent him to Egypt as a slave. But God was with Joseph. God saved many people through Joseph.

Now, use your imagination, as we journey back through time to look at the story, "Joseph: Something Good."

(Story adapted from Genesis 37, 39 to 45, 50:20)

My name is Joseph. I am excited to share with you how God worked in my life.

In Joseph Part 1, I told you how my brothers were so jealous of me that they sold me to some traders traveling to Egypt. My brothers lied to my father and told him that a wild animal had killed me. But I was alive. A man named Potiphar bought me as his slave, but because God was with me, He gave me success in everything I did—even when I ended up in prison for several years. At this point in my story, I was the second-highest official in Egypt because God helped me explain the Pharaoh's dreams. The king's dreams meant that God would bring seven years of plenty and seven years of hunger to Egypt. I suggested that the king put someone in charge to gather and store food during the seven years of plenty. The king chose me!

For seven years, I gathered and stored food in the cities of Egypt. I couldn't measure it—there was so much! Then the seven years of hunger came. The hunger spread to other lands. My father, Jacob, told ten of my brothers to go to Egypt to buy grain. When they arrived, they bowed down before me—just like in my dreams long ago! They didn't recognize me! I acted as if I didn't know them, either. They told me about their family (my family). Then I called them spies and put them in prison. After three days, I told them to leave one brother in Egypt and not to come back without the youngest brother, Benjamin. I wanted to see whether their heart attitudes had changed. I also wanted to see Benjamin.

My servants filled my brothers' bags with grain and secretly included their money. When my brothers found the money, they were afraid. They wondered what God had done to them. Have you ever blamed God for something that happened to you?

Later, my father asked my brothers to go back to Egypt to get more food. Jacob agreed to send Benjamin with them. Jacob knew he might not see any of his sons again, but he trusted God with this. My brothers brought gifts and twice as much money as before. They admitted to finding the money in their sacks the first time, and they tried to give it back.

I cried when I saw Benjamin. Then we ate together.

I sent them home with grain and all their money. I also asked my servant to put my silver cup into Benjamin's sack and then accuse my brothers of stealing it. I wanted to see if their heart attitudes had changed. My brothers agreed that the one who had the cup would become my slave. Benjamin had the cup. My brothers showed their sadness by tearing their clothes.

They returned to my house and said that their father would die if Benjamin didn't return. They couldn't go home without him. My brothers begged to stay as slaves in Benjamin's place. At that point, I knew that my brothers' heart attitudes had changed. I told them that I was Joseph. Then I cried so loudly that everyone in the palace heard me. I told them that God had sent me here ahead of them to save people's lives. What they meant for evil against me, God meant for good.

Let's thank God that He cares for us. Pray these words of praise to Him:

God, thank You that You are with me. You can give me success in everything I do. You show kindness to me. I can't do anything on my own, but You can help many people through me. Thank You that You can make good things happen when others try to hurt me.

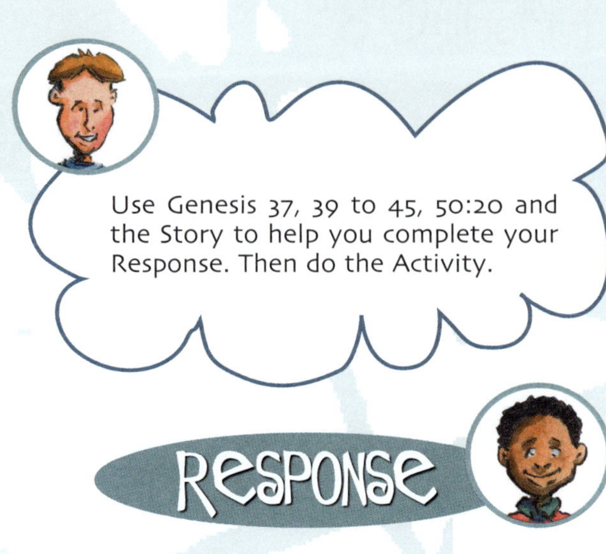

Use Genesis 37, 39 to 45, 50:20 and the Story to help you complete your Response. Then do the Activity.

Response

1. Joseph dreamed that his brothers would _____ _______________.

a. bow down to him
b. sell him as a slave
c. become his slaves

2. How did Joseph's dreams come true when his brothers came to Egypt? ______________

3. Why do you think Joseph spoke to his brothers harshly and tested them when they came to Egypt? (Hint: What did Joseph want to find out about his brothers' heart attitudes?) __________

4. People meant to do evil against Joseph, but God meant it for good. In other words, God made good things happen when others tried to hurt Joseph. Joseph's brothers sold him. Joseph worked as a slave in Potiphar's house. How did God give Joseph success? ______________

5. Potiphar's wife lied, and Joseph went to prison. How did God give Joseph success? (Hint: Think about the prison warden and the king's servants.)

6. Read these verses: "God sent me before you to preserve [save] life . . . you meant evil against me; but God meant it for good . . . to save many people alive" (Genesis 45:5, 50:20).

Now write a letter to God or draw a picture about a time that someone hurt you, but something good came out of it. Thank God that He can make good things happen when people hurt us. Praise Him for His creativity. No one can keep God from carrying out His plans!

Young Children: Draw a picture of Joseph with his brothers.

Good Things Out of Trouble

God saved many people through Joseph. Every time Joseph had trouble, God worked it out and brought something good out of it. God is amazing! When others hurt us, God can bring good out of it! God can make all things work together for our good. No one can keep God from carrying out His plans.

Think about some of your troubles. Then think about the good things that God can bring out of your troubles. Write some of those good things below.

____

____

____

____

____

____

____

____

Episode 9

Moses: His Power, Not Mine

Has someone ever asked you to do something that you felt unsure about? How did you respond?

God's people, the Israelites, were slaves in Egypt. God was concerned about them and wanted to rescue them. He wanted to give them their own land. So God asked a man named Moses to go to the king of Egypt. God wanted Moses to ask the king to release the people. But Moses wasn't so sure about doing this.

Now, use your imagination, as we journey back through time to look at the story, "Moses: His Power, Not Mine."

Story

(Story adapted from Exodus 1 to 4)

My name is Moses. I am excited to share with you how God worked in my life.

The Israelites were Abraham's descendents through his son Isaac. Isaac's son Israel (also called Jacob) and his family moved to Egypt. Israel had seventy people in his family. But 430 years later, about two million Israelites lived in Egypt! Pharaoh (the king of Egypt) feared that the Israelites might attack the Egyptians and leave the country. So the Egyptians made the Israelites work as slaves. God's people suffered terribly. God had promised to give the Israelites their own, good land. He always keeps His promises.

God had a plan for me from the time I was a baby. Pharaoh told the nurses to kill all the newborn Israelite boys. But the nurses trusted God and let the babies live. (I was one of those babies.) Then Pharaoh told the Egyptians to throw every newborn Israelite boy into the Nile River. I also ended up in the Nile River—by a different way. My mother made a basket and put me in it. Then she put the basket into the Nile River. My sister stayed nearby.

Pharaoh's daughter found the basket. She wanted me as her son, but she needed someone to take care of me. So my sister went and got my mother.

Pharaoh's daughter paid my mother to take care of me! My mother cared for me until I could eat solid food. Then Pharaoh's daughter adopted me. I was an Israelite, but I grew up as an Egyptian in Pharaoh's family.

Years later, I saw an Egyptian man beating an Israelite man—one of my people. I killed the Egyptian. I thought I could use my power to help my people. After all, I was Pharaoh's grandson. The next day, I tried to break up a fight between two Israelites, but they didn't want my help. They didn't even respect my power. One of them said, "Who made you our judge? You're not the boss of us." Then he asked whether I planned to kill him, too. Now everyone knew that I had killed an Egyptian! I had to get out of Egypt—fast. I ran away to live in the land of Midian. In Midian, I got married and worked as a shepherd. For forty years, I took care of my father-in-law's sheep.

One day, I came to the mountain of Sinai. A bush was on fire, but the flames did not burn up the bush. Amazing! I had to get a closer look. An angel of the Lord called to me from the flames coming out of the bush. The Lord said that He had seen the Israelites' suffering and was concerned about them. He wanted me to represent Him and bring His people out of Egypt. Me? I was not a great man, but God said He would be with me. I wanted proof, though. What if the Israelites didn't believe that God had appeared to me? God said to tell them that "I AM WHO I AM" sent me to them. That is God's name. He is the Eternal One—the One who has always been.

Then God asked me to throw down my walking stick. It was my most important tool as a shepherd. God wanted me to give up my life as a shepherd and trust Him. When the walking stick hit the ground, it became a snake. I ran! Then God told me to grab the snake by the tail. I did it, and it turned into a walking stick again. God also gave me other miracles. Maybe the people would listen and believe when they saw the miracles.

I still wasn't convinced, though. I never could speak well or find the right words. God reminded me that He made my mouth. He would speak through me. I begged God to send someone else. He said that He would give me the words, and my brother Aaron would speak for me. God wanted me to trust Him. His power, not mine, would bring the people out of Egypt.

Let's thank God that He is the Eternal One, the One who has always been. Pray these words of praise to Him:

Dear God, You promised to give the Israelites their own, good land. You had a plan for Moses from the time he was a baby. Thank You for always remembering Your promises and keeping them. Thank You for having a plan for me.

Use Exodus 1 to 4 and the Story to help you complete your Response. Then do the Activity.

1. Israel (Jacob) had seven people in his family.

   ❑ True ❑ False

2. In what ways did Moses try to use his power to help his people? ______________________

   ____

   Did it work? __________ How do you know? ______________________

   ____

3. It was hard for Moses to trust God at the burning bush. Can you name some things that Moses was worried about? ______________________

   ____

4. God wanted Moses to ________________ ________________ to rescue the Israelites from slavery in Egypt.
a. work hard
b. beg the Pharaoh
c. trust Him

5. God wanted Moses to trust Him instead of ____.
a. himself
b. Aaron
c. Pharaoh
d. All of the above

6. Circle the correct word in each of the parentheses. (God's, Moses') power, not (God's, Moses') power, would bring the people out of Egypt.

7. Read these verses: "But Moses said to God, 'Who am I that I should go to Pharaoh, and that I should bring the children of Israel out of Egypt?' So He said, 'I will certainly be with you'" (Exodus 3:11–12).

Moses didn't think he could help his people. He didn't understand that God's power, not Moses' power, would bring the people out of Egypt. Write a letter to God or draw a picture about a time someone asked you to do something impossible. How did it make you feel? Could God have done it? Praise God for His power. Thank Him that He stays with His people.

Young Children: Draw a picture of Moses at the burning bush.

God's Rescue Message

To discover God's rescue message, unscramble the letters and place them in the spaces. (Use the chart below.)

_ __ __ __ __ __ __ __ __ __ __ __ __
Z L K W E Q M R H A F R P

__ __ __ __ __ __ __ __ __ __
N L J W H P V W K Q

A	B	C	D	E	F	G	H	I	J	K	L	M	N	O	P	Q	R	S	T	U	V	W	X	Y	Z
L	D	N	A	Q	X	B	E	Z	G	T	M	K	J	R	S	U	H	V	W	P	O	Y	I	F	C

Episode 10

Moses: Rescued

Have you ever been afraid to stand up in front of a group of people and speak? What did you do to calm down your nerves?

God wanted Moses to talk to the king of Egypt about freeing His people from slavery. He promised to give Moses the words to say, but Moses was afraid to talk to the king. God wanted Moses to trust Him. It was God's power, not Moses' power that would bring the people out of Egypt.

Now, use your imagination, as we journey back through time to look at the story, "Moses: Rescued."

(Story adapted from Exodus 5 to 14)

My name is Moses. I am excited to share with you how God worked in my life.

In Moses Part 1, I told you how the Egyptians made the Israelites work as slaves. God's people were suffering a lot. The king of Egypt was cruel, and he was starting to be worried about how quickly the Israelites were multiplying. He wondered if they might try to attack the Egyptians and leave the country.

Remember, I was an Israelite, but I grew up as an Egyptian in Pharaoh's family. When I was about forty years old, I killed an Egyptian who was mistreating one of my people. Pharaoh found out about it and tried to kill me. So I ran away to live in the land of Midian, where I got married and worked as a shepherd. For forty years, I took care of my father-in-law's sheep.

Then, one day, God asked me to represent Him and bring His people out of Egypt. He had seen the Israelites' suffering and was concerned about them. He said He would be with me and give me the words to say to the Israelites and to Pharaoh. My brother Aaron would speak for me. God wanted me to trust Him. His power, not mine, would bring the people out of Egypt.

Aaron and I told the Israelites everything that

God had told me. When they heard that God was concerned about them, the Israelites bowed down and worshiped Him.

Pharaoh, however, did not know God and did not want to listen to Him. So the Egyptians beat the Israelites and made them work harder than ever. The Israelites blamed me for their troubles. Suddenly, they didn't want to be rescued—not if it meant extra suffering! I prayed, "God, why have the Israelites' troubles gotten worse? Why haven't You rescued them yet?"

God said to tell the Israelites that He would save them from slavery and make them free by His great power. The Israelites would be His people, and He would be their God. He would lead them to the land He promised to Abraham and his descendents. I told the Israelites these things, but because their slavery was hard, they felt discouraged.

God wanted Pharaoh to know that He is the Lord and that no one is like Him. So God sent ten plagues on the Egyptians. First, He turned all the water in Egypt to blood. Then He sent armies of frogs, gnats, and flies. After that, He sent diseases on the Egyptian farm animals. Then He sent skin sores, hail, locusts, and darkness. After some of the plagues, Pharaoh promised to let the people go, but then he changed his mind again.

Finally, God said that each Israelite family needed to roast a lamb and put its blood on the door frame of their house. Then God went through Egypt and killed every firstborn animal and son. Even Pharaoh's firstborn son died. But God passed over every house that had the blood of the lamb on the door frame. No one died in those houses.

Pharaoh told me to take the Israelites away. Then God led us out of Egypt. He went ahead of us in a pillar of cloud during the day and a pillar of fire at night. But Pharaoh changed his mind again! God wanted Pharaoh and the Israelites to know that He is God and that only He had rescued the Israelites. He wanted the Israelites to trust Him and know that He is in control. So when Pharaoh's army came after us, God split the Red Sea, and the Israelites walked across the sea on dry land. The Egyptian army chased us, but God made the waters come over them, and they all drowned. The Israelites saw God's power, and they trusted Him.

God loved us. He was concerned about us. He wanted us as His people. He fought to have us. He rescued us. He made plans for us. God still loves and pursues people. He makes good plans for them. He wants people to trust in Him.

Let's thank God that He always makes a way for His children. Pray these words of praise to Him:

God, You promised to lead the Israelites to a good land. You planned their rescue from slavery. Your power brought them out of Egypt. They saw Your power and trusted You. Thank You for always keeping Your promises.

Use Exodus 5 to 14 and the Story to help you complete your Response. Then do the Activity.

1. When they heard that God was concerned about them, the Israelites bowed down and worshiped Him.

   ❏ True ❏ False

2. When Pharaoh made the Israelites work harder, they blamed Moses. Why? ___________

   ____

3. God sent ________ plagues on the Egyptians.

4. God told Moses that each Israelite family needed to roast a lamb and put its blood on the door frame of their house. Then God went through Egypt and killed every firstborn animal and son. But God ________________ ___________ every house that had the blood of the lamb on the doorframe. No one died in those houses.

5. God wanted the people to trust Him and know that He is _____ __________________. Can you name some ways God showed His power so that the Israelites would trust Him? _____________
____

6. Read this verse: "Now the blood shall be a sign for you on the houses where you are. And when I see the blood, I will pass over you" (Exodus 12:13).

Write a letter to God or draw a picture about a time you cried because you were suffering. Do you think God hears you when you cry? Do you think He is concerned about you? In what ways do you need "rescuing?" Tell God about it. He'll listen.

Young Children: Draw a picture about the Red Sea splitting apart for the Israelites to walk on dry ground.

Cloud and Fire Mazes

God brought the Israelites out of Egypt. He went ahead of them in a pillar of cloud during the day and a pillar of fire at night. Why?

Follow the pillar of cloud through the first maze and the pillar of fire through the second maze. Write the letters you come to on the lines below.

"The LORD went before them by day in a pillar of cloud _______ _________ ________ ________, and by night in a pillar of fire _______ _________ _________ _________" (Exodus 13:21).

Episode 11

Moses: Dependent

Do you complain when things don't go your way? How do you react when you make a plan, but it doesn't play out the way you thought it would?

When Moses led the Israelites out of Egypt, they saw big miracles all along the way. But they soon started to complain because God's plan was different than their plan.

Now, use your imagination, as we journey back through time to look at the story, "Moses: Dependent."

(Story adapted from Exodus 15 to 20)

My name is Moses. I am excited to share with you how God worked in my life.

In Moses, Part 1, I told you how God protected me as a newborn baby, floating down the Nile River in a little basket. After many years as a shepherd in Midian, God came to me in the midst of a burning bush and told me He wanted me to lead the Israelites out of their slavery in Egypt.

I made all kinds of excuses why I wasn't the right man for this job, but God wanted me to trust Him, not myself, as I led His people out of Egypt. In Moses, Part 2, I shared about the plagues and how God showed His mighty power, and I explained how the tradition of the Passover came to be part of Jewish history.

God was faithful to His promise and after many miracles, He led us out of Egypt. He went ahead of us in a pillar of cloud during the day and a pillar of fire at night. Pharaoh's army came after us, but God split the Red Sea, and the Israelites walked across the sea on dry land. The Egyptian army chased us, but God made the waters come over them, and they all drowned. The Israelites saw God's power against the Egyptians, and they trusted God.

Yet, once we got into the desert, the people started complaining. They were hungry. They cried, "It would have been better if God had killed us in Egypt. At least while we were slaves, we had plenty of food! You have brought us out here to die!" They were afraid that God had forgotten about food! God had used His great power against the Egyptians. The Israelites had seen God's power and trusted Him. God had made detailed plans for their rescue. Yet, when the Israelites felt afraid, they forgot the ways that God had taken care of them, and they had trouble depending upon Him.

Each day, God sent bread from the sky and flocks of quail (a kind of bird). We gathered quail in the evening and the bread in the morning, six days a week. Some people tried to stock up for the next day, but the food always rotted. God wanted us to depend upon Him to send food each day. The sixth day of each week, we gathered twice as much food. God wanted us to rest on the seventh day, just like He did after creating the world. The food didn't rot on the seventh day. Some people tried to gather food on the seventh day anyway, but God didn't send food that day. God took care of us.

Three months after we crossed the Red Sea, we arrived at Mount Sinai. God gave me some instructions, including the Ten Commandments and other laws. Yet, we discovered that we could not measure up to God's perfect requirements, no matter how hard we tried. God wanted us to depend upon Him instead of upon ourselves. Our "not measuring up" meant "to sin."

God wanted us to sacrifice an animal when we sinned. God chose some people as priests. The priests offered the animal's blood on the altar. We sacrificed animals continually. Only the blood of the Promised Lamb could—once and for all—take away sins. We looked forward to His coming. By trusting in Him, we could have forgiveness for sins and escape eternal death. God would send the Promised Lamb 1,500 years later.

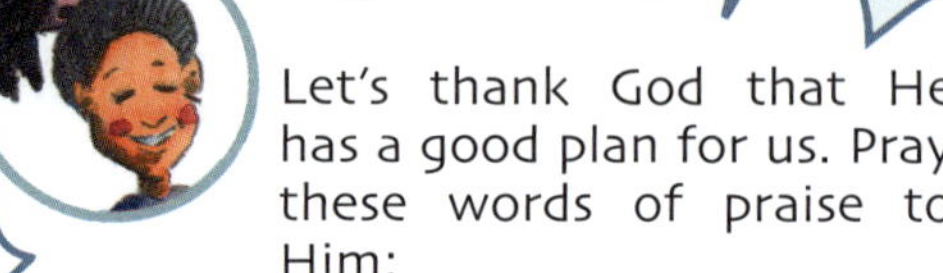

Let's thank God that He has a good plan for us. Pray these words of praise to Him:

God, You rescued the Israelites from slavery. You took care of them in the desert. You wanted them to depend upon You. Thank You for loving me. Thank You for making a way for people to have forgiveness for sins and escape eternal death.

Use Exodus 15 to 20 and the Story to help you complete your Response. Then do the Activity.

RESPONSE

1. God made detailed plans for the Israelites' rescue. (Imagine planning an escape for two million people!) God used His great power against the Egyptians. The Israelites saw God's power and trusted Him. Yet, when the Israelites got hungry in the desert, they got worried. They started complaining and stopped depending upon God. Why? (Circle as many responses below as you want, and write some of your own.)

a. They forgot how God had taken care of them in the past.

b. They didn't believe that God had good plans for them.

c. They wanted to be in control. They didn't understand that God was in control—and that He would take good care of them.

d. (What do you think?) ____________________

e. (What do you think?) ____________________

2. Can you name some ways that God took care of His people in the desert?

____

____

3. God gave the Ten Commandments and other laws to Moses. The people could not ______________________ to God's perfect requirements, no matter how hard they tried.

4. Why would God give laws that the people couldn't follow on their own?

____

____

5. Read this verse: "'You have seen what I did to the Egyptians, and how I bore you on eagles' wings and brought you to Myself" (Exodus 19:4).

God carried the Israelites out of Egypt as an eagle carries her young on her wings. God protected the people during the rescue. They were never in danger. He brought them to Him. Write a letter to God or draw a picture about a time that you thought you were in danger but found out that someone had been protecting you. Thank God for caring for you.

Young Children: Draw a picture of Moses with the Ten Commandments.

Measuring Up

Look at the chart below. It contains the Ten Commandments that God gave to Moses and the people of Israel. Do you try to keep the Ten Commandments? Have you kept any of them perfectly? Color the squares next to the commandments that you have always kept (and never broken). Be honest!

- ☐ 10. Do not want what other people have.
- ☐ 9. Tell the truth about people.
- ☐ 8. Do not steal.
- ☐ 7. Promise to stay faithful to your husband or wife (when you are a grown-up).
- ☐ 6. Do not murder, or even hate, anyone. God is the Life Giver. Respect the life that He gives each person.
- ☐ 5. Honor your father and mother.
- ☐ 4. Keep God's day special and holy.
- ☐ 3. Do not misuse God's name.
- ☐ 2. Do not make or worship any idols (e.g., grades, money, clothes, toys, popularity, friends, etc.).
- ☐ 1. Worship God only.

What did you find out about yourself? No one can be good enough for God, no matter how hard he or she tries. Why would God give us laws that we can't keep? To lead us to trust in His Promised One—the only One who ever measured up. He has done the measuring up for us! By trusting in Him, we share in His goodness. When He comes to live in us, we become like Him and show His glory. In fact, the Promised One is our only hope for glory.

Episode 12

Joshua: Courageous Trust

Have you ever wondered why God does things the way He does? The book of Isaiah tells us that God's ways are not like our ways, and His thoughts are not like our thoughts. That's because He's God and we're not.

That's how it was for Joshua. He was a military leader. He had won many battles with God's intervention. But the way God told him to conquer Jericho didn't use any type of military strategy. It didn't make any sense. The good thing about Joshua was, he knew God well enough to trust Him—even when it didn't make any sense.

Now, use your imagination, as we journey back through time to look at the story, "Joshua: Courageous Trust."

(Story adapted from the book of Joshua)

My name is Joshua. I am excited to share with you how God worked in my life.

I was Moses' assistant when he led the Israelites out of Egypt. After Moses died, God wanted me to lead His people into the land that He had promised to give them. Just as He was with Moses, God promised He would always be with us on the journey. As soon as I started to lead, three times God told me to be strong and brave, and He promised that I would be successful in everything that I did. He wanted me to trust Him.

I sent two spies to Jericho to look at the land and give me a report. Somehow, the king of Jericho heard about my spies, so they looked for a place to hide. God led them to the house of a woman named Rahab. Her house was built on the city wall, so they climbed out a window and scaled the wall, using a red rope. Rahab told them to go into the hills because the king's men would not find them there. Then she asked my men to promise that if they returned to capture the city, they would show kindness to her family just as she had been kind to them. They agreed and told her to tie the same red rope in that window. It would be the sign to keep everyone safe in her house.

The two men came back and reported that all the people in Jericho were terribly afraid of us. They had heard how God dried up the Red Sea when we came out of Egypt. They were afraid because they knew that our God, the one true God, ruled the heavens above and the earth below.

The next morning, we traveled to the Jordan River to cross into Jericho and capture the city. During harvest the Jordan River flooded, so the river was at its fullest. But when the priests stepped into the water, it stopped flowing. After we all crossed the river, the water began flowing again. It overflowed its banks, just as it had before we crossed it. God did the same miracle for us that He had done at the Red Sea. When we set up camp, we stacked twelve large rocks in a pile to remind us of God's great power and His protection.

The people of Jericho were so afraid of us they had guards at the city gates. No one went into the city and no one came out. By now, the Lord had assured me that He had already given Jericho into our hands, and then He gave me some really strange orders. He told me to march my army around the city one time every day for six days. Seven trumpets played continuously while we marched. But no one was to speak until the seventh day when we marched around the city seven times. As soon as the trumpets made one long blast, we all gave a shout. At that very moment, the city walls came tumbling down and we captured Jericho. And as we promised, Rahab's family was safe.

Many years later, I called a meeting and recalled the many victories God had given us over our enemies. I encouraged the people to love God with all their hearts and not turn against Him. I reminded them that God gave us the land that we didn't cultivate and cities that we didn't build. We ate from vineyards and olive trees that we didn't plant. I believe people need physical reminders so we don't forget God's care. We put a large stone near the Lord's Holy Tent to remind everyone of God's power and protection.

Let's thank God for His great power and protection. Pray these words of praise to Him:

God, thank You for Your love and care for us. Thank You that even when our circumstances don't make any sense to us, we can trust You because You can see the big picture.

Use the book of Joshua and the Story to help you complete your Response. Then do the Activity.

1. After Moses died, God wanted Joshua to lead His people into the land that He had promised to give them.

❑ True ❑ False

2. Rahab's house was built on the city wall, so the spies climbed out a window and scaled the wall, using a ______________________.

a. ladder
b. red rope
c. pile of rocks

3. When Joshua and the people set up camp, they stacked twelve large rocks in a pile to remind them of God's great ______________ and His ______________________.

4. By now, the Lord had assured Joshua that He had already given Jericho into their hands, and then He gave Joshua some really ____.

a. good food
b. strange orders
c. powerful weapons

5. Joshua encouraged the people to __________ God with all their ____________________ and not turn against Him.

6. Read this verse: "Be strong and of good courage; do not be afraid, nor be dismayed, for the LORD your God is with you wherever you go" (Joshua 1:9).

Now write a letter to God or draw a picture about a time you felt God was with you. Did you feel less fearful?

Young Children: Draw a picture of the walls of Jericho when they came crashing down.

STRANGE INSTRUCTIONS

God gave Joshua some strange instructions to conquer the city of Jericho, but Joshua knew God. See if you can solve the puzzle phrase below. (Hint: The letters in the filled–in blanks are not used again.)

A B C D E F G H I J K L M N O P Q R S T U V W X Y Z

_o_h_a t___te_ _o_, e_en

_hen it _i_n't ma_e _en_e.

Episode 13

Samson: It's Never Too Late

Have you ever been determined to do something, but obstacles kept getting in your way? How did you respond?

Samson, a one-man military leader, was determined to defeat his enemy, but obstacles kept getting in his way. God used his life—and death—to bring about Israel's deliverance from the Philistines.

Now, use your imagination, as we journey back through time to look at the story, "Samson: It's Never Too Late."

Story

(Story adapted from Judges 13 to 16)

My name is Samson. I am excited to share with you how God worked in my life.

Years after God used Moses to deliver the Israelites from Egyptian slavery, God allowed the Philistines to rule over Israel for 40 years. During that time, my mother could not have children, but the angel of the Lord promised her a son. He said I would be a Nazirite (one given to God) from the womb to my death, and I would deliver my people from the Philistines. It's amazing that God is always working behind the scenes to accomplish His purpose—even when we don't understand.

The Lord blessed me, and the Spirit of the Lord came upon me with great power. One time when a lion came roaring towards me, I tore the lion apart with my bare hands. Another time, I killed 1,000 men with a donkey's jawbone. Many more times in my life the Spirit of the Lord gave me unusual power against the Philistines. And every time they saw the great power of the Lord in my life, they tried to trick me into telling them where my power came from.

Later in my life, I fell in love with a Philistine woman named Delilah. Each of the Philistine rulers promised Delilah eleven hundred pieces of silver if she could trick me into revealing where my

great strength came from so they could capture me. So Delilah asked me where my strength came from, and I told her that if they used seven new bowstrings that had not been dried, then I would become weak and be like any other man. The rulers of the Philistines brought Delilah seven new bowstrings, and she tied me up when I was asleep. She had men hiding in another room, and then she said, "The Philistines are upon you!" I easily broke the bowstrings, and the secret of my strength was not discovered. Two more times she asked me to tell her the secret of my strength, but both times I easily got free.

Delilah wouldn't stop asking me about my secret, and finally I told her the truth. If someone shaved my head, then I would lose my strength. Delilah called for the Philistine rulers again. The money was more important to her than I was, so when I was asleep, one of the men shaved off the seven braids of my hair. When I awoke and saw the Philistines, I thought I would get free like the other times, but my strength had left me—my hair was gone. The Philistines captured me, gouged out my eyes, put me in prison, and made me grind grain like an ox.

The rulers of the Philistines praised their false god for giving me into their hands. Throughout my time in prison, they often paraded me out of the jail like a war trophy to entertain them. One time, they made me stand between the pillars that held up the temple, which was full of about three thousand men and women. The Philistine rulers were there too. By this time, my hair had grown back, so I prayed to the Lord God and asked Him to give me strength one more time. I asked Him to let me die with the Philistines. I grabbed the two middle pillars on which the temple rested, and I pushed as hard as I could with my right hand and my left hand. The whole temple collapsed. I killed more of our enemies at my death than I killed during my lifetime.

I had many failures, but the Lord still worked mightily through my life. Even though I didn't always act like a Nazirite, it didn't change the fact that I was given to God from the day I was born until the day I died. God fulfilled His purposes in my life and in my death.

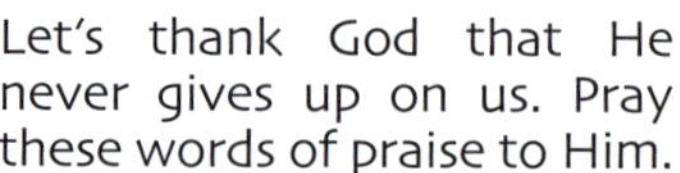

Let's thank God that He never gives up on us. Pray these words of praise to Him.

God, thank You that in spite of my failures, You still want to work mightily through my life. Even though I may not always act like one given to God, once I'm Yours, my behavior can never change that fact. God, thank You that You will fulfill Your purposes in my life.

Use Judges 13 to 16 and the Story to help you complete your Response. Then do the Activity.

1. Samson would be a Nazirite (one given to God) from the womb to his death.

❑ True ❑ False

2. One time when a lion came roaring towards Samson, He tore the lion apart with his ______________________. Many more times in his life the _________ ____ ______ ___________ gave him unusual power.

3. When Samson awoke and saw the Philistines, he thought he would get free like the other times, but his ______________________ had left him—his _____________ was gone.

4. Samson prayed to the Lord God and asked Him to give him ____________________ one more time.
a. wisdom
b. strength
c. victory

5. Read this verse: "For the child shall be a Nazirite to God from the womb to the day of his death" (Judges 13:7).

Now write a letter to God or draw a picture about a time God gave you extra strength to do something that was hard for you to do. You knew God was in this because you couldn't do it by yourself.

Young Children: Draw a picture of Samson standing between the two pillars of the temple.

RIDDLES

You can read a riddle that Samson made up in Judges 14:14. See if you can answer these riddles from today's lesson.

The angel of the Lord appeared,
To announce the birth of a son.
The angel's instructions were very clear,
Samson's role was "one given to God."

What was the name given to people who were dedicated to God? ______________________________

The Spirit of the Lord worked through Samson,
The secret to his strength kept him free,
The power was in the roots, a strange place indeed.

What was the secret to Samson's strength? ______________________________

Episode 14

Ruth: A New Life

Have you ever moved to a new place, where you didn't know anyone? Who noticed you and accepted you? Who helped you? Who became your friends?

Ruth moved to a new land. Her husband had died, so she clung to her mother–in–law, Naomi. Then God brought a new person to take care of Ruth.

Now, use your imagination, as we journey back through time to look at the story, "Ruth: A New Life."

(Story adapted from the book of Ruth)

My name is Ruth. I am excited to share with you how God worked in my life.

I am from the land of Moab, but I remember a time when the land of Israel did not have enough food. A woman named Naomi, her husband, and their two sons lived in Bethlehem, Israel. They moved to Moab to find food. After a while, Naomi's husband died. I married one of her sons, and we stayed in Moab for ten years. Then my husband and his brother also died. Naomi decided to leave Moab and go back to Bethlehem. She had heard that God had provided food to Israel. I wanted to go with Naomi, but she told me to go home. She said that she couldn't help me find a new husband. We cried, and I clung to Naomi. I did not want her to go without me. Finally, she let me go with her to Israel.

Naomi had a wealthy relative named Boaz. He lived in Israel. One day, I went into the fields to gather grain that the workers had left behind. I went into Boaz's field. He noticed me and asked who I was. He told me to stay in his field, gather grain, and get water when I was thirsty. I bowed before Boaz. I asked him why I had found favor in his eyes and why he noticed me. I was a foreigner!

Boaz said that he knew I had left my father, mother, and country, so he would provide for me. He had seen me at my worst. I was all dirty from working in the field, yet he accepted me. He even invited me to come and eat with him. Boaz is like the Promised One. The Promised One invites all people to come to Him. He accepts them, no matter how dirty they appear.

I gathered grain in Boaz's field until the harvest was finished. Naomi thought that Boaz might want to take care of me or even marry me. So she told me to clean myself up and go to Boaz. I waited until Boaz fell asleep beside a pile of grain. Then I quietly laid down at his feet. About midnight, Boaz woke up. Startled, he asked who I was. I told him my name and asked him to take care of me. According to Jewish customs, if a husband died, the closest male relative took care of his wife. Boaz blessed me and said that he would take care of me—and even marry me—if Naomi's closest relative refused to take care of me.

Boaz found the relative. He told him that Naomi wanted to sell a piece of land that had belonged to her husband. If the relative bought the land, then he had to marry me. The relative said he couldn't do this. He told Boaz to buy the land and took off his sandal. Long ago in Israel, when people traded or bought back something, one person took off his sandal and gave it to the other person. This was their "proof of purchase." Boaz told the leaders and all the people that he had bought everything that belonged to Naomi's husband. He also said that he would marry me. The leaders and all the people blessed us, saying, "May you prosper . . . and be famous in Bethlehem." Boaz bought the land back for me. Then Boaz and I married. God enabled me to become pregnant, and I gave birth to a son. The women said to Naomi, "May he be famous in Israel! And may he give you new life."

I'm so glad that Boaz wanted me. He made me part of his family. He took care of me. He gave me a new life.

Let's thank God that He accepts us just the way we are. Pray these words of praise to Him:

God, Thank You for noticing me and providing for me. You give me everything I need. You take care of me. I want to know You as my Life Giver.

Use the book of Ruth and the Story to help you complete your Response. Then do the Activity.

1. Ruth clung to Naomi. Ruth did not want Naomi to go without her.

❑ True ❑ False

2. Boaz saw Ruth at her worst. She was all dirty from working in the field, yet he _______________ her.

a. rejected
b. accepted
c. looked down on

3. In what ways did Boaz take care of Ruth?

____

____

4. According to Jewish customs, if a husband died, the closest male relative took care of his wife. Boaz blessed Ruth and said that he would take care of her—and even marry her—if Naomi's closest relative refused to take care of her. What did Boaz buy back so he could marry Ruth?

____

____

5. Ruth gave birth to a son. The women said to Naomi, "May he be famous in Israel! And may he give you _______________ ____________________."

6. Read this verse: "For wherever you go, I will go; and wherever you lodge, I will lodge; your people shall be my people, and your God, my God" (Ruth 1:16).

Pretend that you are an adopted child. (If you are an adopted child, then this exercise is not make-believe for you.) Write a letter to your parents. Thank them for wanting you and accepting you. Thank them for making you a part of their family. Then list the ways your parents take care of you, and thank them for those things. Thank them for the new life they gave you.

Young Children: Think of three ways your parents take care of you.

ADOPTION

Solve the crossword puzzle below. Use the words in the word box.

- redeem
- adopts
- family
- grace
- restores
- foreigner

Imagine that you have lost your entire family, become an orphan, and moved to a new and strange place. You are all alone and have no one. Who will take care of you? You meet a wealthy, kind relative named Joshua. Joshua wants to adopt you! He will give you everything you need. He will love you and take good care of you. Complete your adoption certificate below, using all six words from the crossword puzzle.

ADOPTION CERTIFICATE

[your name] ____________________ is a ____________________.

Joshua has shown ____________________________ to [your name] ____________________________________.

Joshua chooses to ____________________ [your name] ____________________ and his/her family's property.

Joshua accepts [your name] ____________________ and promises to give

[your name] ______________________ everything he/she needs.

On this day, Joshua ____________________ and ____________________ [your name] ____________________.

[your name] ____________________________ is now part of Joshua's ____________________________________.

Episode 15

David: Conquering Our Giants

Has something or someone ever challenged you in your life, and you've seen how you were uniquely prepared to meet this challenge?

David totally depended upon God to meet his challenges. God anointed David as the next king of Israel. God also prepared him to defeat his enemy.

Now, use your imagination, as we journey back through time to look at the story, "David: Conquering Our Giants."

Story

(Story adapted from I Samuel 16 to 17)

My name is David. I am excited to share with you how God worked in my life.

I grew up in the town of Bethlehem, Israel, with my father, Jesse, and my seven older brothers. When I was a teenager, King Saul was Israel's first king, but he rejected God. So God decided to choose a new king—someone who loved God and depended upon Him. God told a man named Samuel that one of my father's sons would be the next king. God sent Samuel to Bethlehem, to our family, to choose the next king.

Since I was the youngest, I took care of my father's sheep while my family went to meet Samuel. My oldest brother, Eliab, was tall and handsome, so Samuel thought he would be the next king. But Eliab wasn't God's choice. God told Samuel that people judge others by what they look like, but He judges people by what is in their hearts.

All seven of my brothers passed in front of Samuel, but God didn't choose any of them. Confused, Samuel asked my father, "Are these all your sons?" Then my father told Samuel about his youngest son, me. My father told him I was tending the sheep. Samuel said, "Go get him. We won't sit down until he gets here."

When I arrived, God said to Samuel, "He is the one." Then I knelt in front of Samuel. He put oil on my head as a sign that God had chosen me to be the next king of Israel. But I didn't become king right away. I had to wait a long time. Only God knew when I would become king.

Israel was at war with the Philistine people, and King Saul was with Israel's army. Three of my seven brothers were fighting in the war, so my father sent me to take food and check on them. The Philistines had a champion fighter named Goliath. He stood about nine feet tall! He was a giant! For forty days, he came out and dared any Israelite soldier to fight him. Each time he appeared, all the Israelite soldiers trembled in fear and ran away. When I arrived at my brothers' camp, the soldiers were lining up for battle. Then Goliath came out and dared the Israelite soldiers to fight him. Goliath did not belong to God. Why did he think he could speak against the armies of the living God?

I told King Saul that I would go and fight Goliath, but Saul said I was just a boy. I told Saul that God had prepared me for this battle because I had killed a lion and a bear when they attacked my father's sheep. God saved me from the lion and the bear, and I trusted Him to save me from this giant, too. Goliath would die because he stood against the armies of the living God. Saul blessed me and said I could fight Goliath. Then he put his armor on me, but it was too big and awkward. I took it off and used my slingshot, instead.

I chose five smooth stones from a stream and went out to meet the giant. Goliath moved toward me. I told him that he came to me with a sword, spear, and javelin, but I came to him in the name of the Lord of heaven's armies. I ran toward Goliath, put a stone into my slingshot, and slung it at him. The stone sank into Goliath's forehead, and he fell facedown on the ground. Then I killed him with his own sword. When the Philistines saw that their champion was dead, they turned and ran. Our men chased them and defeated them.

Let's thank God that He is always with us, and we don't need to be afraid. Pray these words of praise to Him:

God, thank You that You can prepare me to overcome any "giant" in my life. I want to love You and depend upon You like David did.

Use I Samuel 16 to 17 and the Story to help you complete your Response. Then do the Activity.

1. David grew up in the town of Bethlehem, Israel.

❑ True ❑ False

2. God decided to choose a new king—someone who ______________ God and ______________ ______________ Him.

3. Eliab wasn't God's choice to be the next king. God told Samuel that people judge others by what they look like, but He judges people by what is in their ______________________.

a. family
b. hearts
c. flocks of sheep

4. David arrived, and God said to Samuel, "He is the ______________________________."

5. Goliath stood about _______________ feet tall! He was a giant!
a. nine
b. four
c. forty

6. All the Israelite soldiers trembled in _______________ and ran away.

7. Goliath came to David with a sword, spear, and javelin. But David came to Goliath in the name of the _____________ _____ ________
_____________________________.

8. David _______________ toward Goliath.
a. walked
b. skipped
c. ran

9. Read this verse: "For the LORD does not see as man sees; for man looks at the outward appearance, but the LORD looks at the heart" (1 Samuel 16:7).

Now write a letter to God or draw a picture about a time you judged someone based on how they looked before you got to know them as a person.

Young Children: Draw a picture of David and Goliath.

David Trusted God

While David was a shepherd, tending his father's sheep, God gave him the extra strength to kill a bear and a lion. When David fought Goliath, he could trust God to give him victory because of his past experiences. Find the words listed below in the puzzle that describe the story

P	Y	L	O	X	R	S	V	E	L
S	L	I	N	G	S	H	O	T	I
F	B	I	Y	Q	A	E	E	M	O
S	E	E	H	S	P	Z	M	N	
C	E	A	A	K	P	H	P	H	O
D	H	N	R	R	P	E	X	T	X
Z	U	S	O	L	P	R	V	S	M
A	P	E	V	T	E	D	H	U	H
F	A	I	T	H	S	S	B	R	P
R	O	I	R	R	A	W	S	T	X

BEAR	LION	STONES
FAITH	SHEPHERD	TRUST
FEARLESS	SLINGSHOT	WARRIOR

Episode 16

David: Day of Discovery

Have you tried to make friends with someone, but he or she did not want to be friends with you? How did that make you feel?

David loved and depended upon God. David wanted to honor and serve the king of Israel, but King Saul was so jealous, he tried to kill David more than once.

Now, use your imagination, as we journey back through time to look at the story, "David: Day of Discovery."

Story

(Story adapted from 1 Samuel 18:1 to 31:13 and the book of 2 Samuel)

My name is David. I am excited to share with you how God worked in my life.

After I killed Goliath the giant, I became such a hero to the Hebrew people that they sang songs about me. King Saul became very jealous of me and even tried to kill me twice with his spear. I escaped both times, but I knew I couldn't trust him. Even when I married Saul's daughter, Michal, he still plotted to kill me.

It was unusual how things worked out, but Saul's son, Jonathan, became my best friend. Jonathan would always warn me about King Saul's plans. He asked his father to let me go, but that made Saul even more furious. He wanted his son Jonathan to become the next king of Israel, not me. But Jonathan knew that God had chosen me to be the next king, so he willingly gave up his right as heir to the throne. He did all he could to help protect my life.

I was afraid so I hid out in different caves. One day, Saul came all by himself into the same cave that I was in. My men believed God had given Saul into my hands, and they wanted me to kill him. But I didn't want to harm the king, even though he wanted to harm me. On another

occasion, I went into Saul's camp at night. The Lord caused Saul and his men to stay asleep while I took his spear and water jug. Again, one of my men wanted me to kill the king, but I wanted to wait on God to give me the kingdom, instead of grabbing it for myself. Is there something in your life that God wants you to wait for Him to give you? Or are you trying to grab it now for yourself?

After Saul died I was made the king of Judah, and eventually I was the king over all of Israel. I won many battles, but in my success I made a huge mistake. Instead of being on the battlefield with my soldiers, I decided to stay at home. One night I saw a beautiful woman who lived near my house. She was the wife of one of my soldiers, and I took her as if she was my wife. Shortly after this, the woman, Bathsheba, told me she was going to have a child by me. Instead of confessing my sin, I tried to hide it. I sent Bathsheba's husband, Uriah, to the fiercest battle so he would get killed.

As a result of my deception in hiding this secret, I suffered for many years in my relationship with my family and friends. The child that was born to Bathsheba died. My eldest son, Absalom, killed my other son, Amnon. Then Absalom got killed while he was trying to take over my kingdom. Confession would have been painful for me, but it would have saved many unnecessary consequences. Have you ever found yourself trying to run away and hide a secret sin in order to avoid the consequences?

My huge mistakes, as well as my great moments, caused me to look for an intimate personal relationship with God. In many of the Psalms, I cried out to God for His deliverance from my enemies and for His mercy on my life. I also wrote many Psalms of praise to God for His love and protection such as, "The Lord is my Shepherd; I have everything I need." The Promised One who would never sin and would take away the sin of the world is truly the King of all kings and the Lord of all lords!

Let's thank God that we can come to Him and confess our sins (instead of trying to hide them). Pray these words of praise to Him:

God, thank You that I can wait on You to give me what I need, instead of grabbing it for myself. I don't have to hide when I am afraid. I know that it is always better to confess my sin than to hide it. Thank You for sending the Promised One to take on the payment for our sins. He truly is the King of all kings and the Lord of all lords!

Use 1 Samuel 18:1 to 31:13, the book of 2 Samuel, and the Story to help you complete your Response. Then do the Activity.

RESPONSE

1. After David killed Goliath the giant, he became such a hero to the Hebrew people that they sang songs about him, which delighted King Saul.

❑ True ❑ False

2. King Saul became very jealous of David and even tried to __________________ him twice with his spear.

a. hit
b. throw
c. kill

3. It was unusual how things worked out, but Saul's son, Jonathan, became David's _________ ___________________________.

4. But Jonathan knew that God had chosen David to be the next king, so he willingly ____ ____ as heir to the throne.

a. held onto his right
b. gave up his right
c. fought for his right

5. __________________________ would have been painful for David, but it would have saved many unnecessary ____________ ____.

6. What did David's huge mistakes, as well as his great moments, cause him to look for with God? ________________________________ ____ ____.

7. The Promised One who would never sin and would take away the sin of the world is truly the ______________________________ ____ ____

8. Read this verse: "And your house and your kingdom shall be established forever before you. Your throne shall be established forever" (2 Samuel 7:16).

Now write a letter to God or draw a picture about a time you wanted to know more about His eternal kingdom.

Young Children: Draw a picture of David sitting on his throne as King of Israel.

GOD'S TIMING

Each letter that is to be inserted in the puzzle grid appears in the same column of letters below the grid. To solve the puzzle, you must choose the correct letter in the column and write it in the puzzle to build a phrase. David is the first word for the top left corner of the puzzle.

- The letter "D" is the only choice in the far left column of letters.

- The next column over, you have a choice between a "T" and an "A" – choose the "A."

- The third column from the left, the choices are "I" – "I" – "O" – "V." Choose the "V" to continue to spell David.

- The fourth column over, you have the choices of "K" – "I" – "M" – "S" – "N" – "B." You would choose the "I."

- The fifth column over you would choose the "D."

Have fun solving the rest of the puzzle!

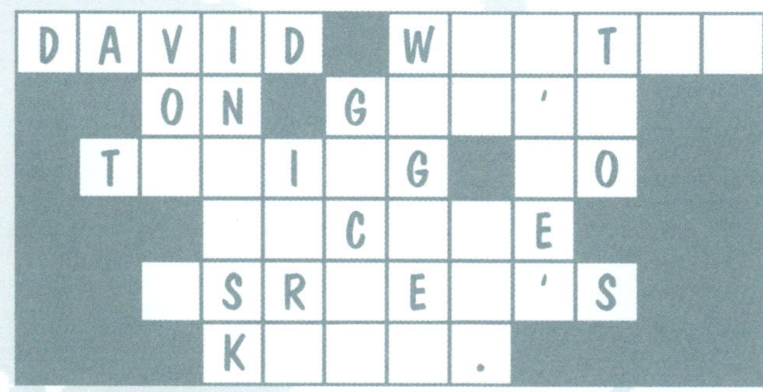

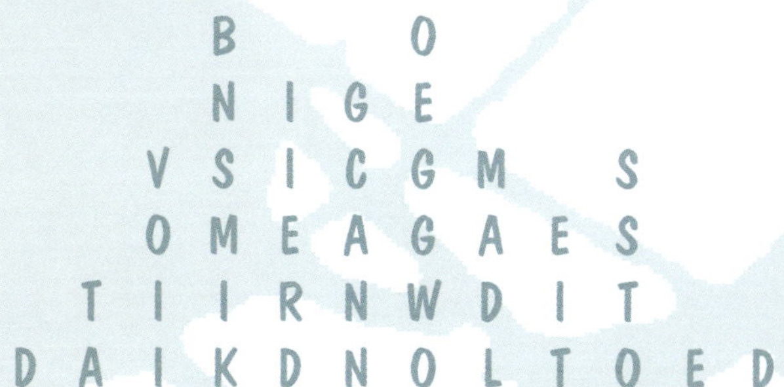

Episode 17

Esther: Trusting God for the Moment at Hand

Try to imagine trusting God enough to step out in faith, even though it might cost you everything—even your life. That's exactly what happened to Esther, but God gave her the courage to risk everything to save her people, the Jews.

When Esther became the queen of Persia, she acted bravely in the face of danger. She trusted God to not only save her life, but all of the Jewish people during King Xerxes' rule.

Now, use your imagination, as we journey back through time to look at the story, "Esther: Trusting God for the Moment at Hand."

Story

(Story adapted from the book of Esther)

My name is Esther. I am excited to share with you how God worked in my life.

King Xerxes gave a banquet for his royal officers that lasted one hundred eighty days. He was showing off his kingdom and his own greatness, and he wanted to show off his beautiful queen too. He commanded his servants to bring Queen Vashti to the banquet, but she refused to come. The king became very angry that she disobeyed his order, so he began to search for a new queen.

Mordecai, my older cousin, adopted me when my father and mother died. Mordecai was a government official, so when he heard about the king's new search, I was sent along with several other young women for the king to see. King Xerxes chose me, and I became Queen Esther.

Soon after, the king honored a man named Haman and ordered all of the royal officials to bow down to him. But my cousin would not bow down to Haman because we were Jewish and believed that only the one true God was to be worshipped. That made Haman angry, so he started looking for a way to destroy all of the Jewish people. Have you ever had to make a stand for what you believed, regardless of the outcome? That's what Mordecai did.

Haman told King Xerxes that the Jewish people would not obey the king's laws. King Xerxes gave Haman the authority to do whatever he pleased. Haman ordered all the Jews to be killed in a single day.

When Mordecai heard this news, he was very upset. He asked me to go to King Xerxes and beg for mercy for our people. Until now, no one knew that I was Jewish except Mordecai. I reminded my cousin that people couldn't go into the king's presence without being called by him. They would be killed (unless the king held out his gold scepter, which meant that person may live). Mordecai gave me some wise counsel that made me think, "Who knows, maybe I have been chosen queen for such a time as this."

I told Mordecai that I would go to the king and risk my life for my people. And if I die, I die. I put on my royal robe and stood facing the king's hall. When the king saw me, he held out the golden scepter. He asked what I wanted. I invited him to come with Haman to a banquet the next day. I would answer his question then.

In the meantime, Haman's wife and friends advised him to hang Mordecai for his disobedience. Haman ordered the "hanging platform" to be built.

That same night the king could not sleep. He ordered that the daily court record be read to him. It was recorded that at one time Mordecai had warned the king about two of his officers who planned to kill the king. King Xerxes asked what reward had been given to Mordecai for protecting the king. His servants answered that nothing had been done.

The next morning, Haman came to tell the king about his plan to hang Mordecai. Not good timing for Haman! Before Haman could ask about the hanging, the king asked Haman what should be done to honor someone. Haman assumed the king was talking about him, so he suggested that the honored man should wear a royal robe that the king himself had worn and ride through the city streets on the king's horse with a royal crown on its head. The king commanded Haman to do all that for Mordecai. That made Haman very angry!

At my banquet, the king asked me what I wanted. He offered to give me up to half of his kingdom. But I asked the king to let all the Jewish people live because there were orders for all of us to be killed. He asked who gave the orders. I answered, "Haman." King Xerxes ordered that Haman be hung on the very platform that he had built for Mordecai.

Then the king ordered that the Jewish people not be killed, and said they had the right to protect themselves from anyone who tried to attack them. Mordecai became second in command to King Xerxes, and he became the most important man among the Jews.

Let's thank God that we can always trust Him to provide the courage we need in any situation. Pray these words of thanks to Him:

God, thank You that we don't have to be afraid. You've promised to never leave us, and we can trust You to provide the courage we need when we have something hard to do. You will be with us just like You were with Mordecai and Esther.

Use the book of Esther and the Story to help you complete your Response. Then do the Activity.

Response

1. King Xerxes commanded his servants to bring Queen Vashti to the banquet, and she came with them.

❑ True ❑ False

2. King Xerxes chose Esther, and she became ____________ ____________.

3. Mordecai would not bow down to Haman because he was Jewish and believed that only the __________ ____________ __________ was to be worshipped.

4. Haman ordered all the Jews to be _________ in a single day.
a. arrested
b. honored
c. killed

5. Esther told Mordecai that she would go to the king and __________ _________ __________ for her people.

6. Read this verse: "Yet who knows whether you have come to the kingdom for such a time as this?" (Esther 4:14).

Now write a letter to God or draw a picture about a time you felt God placed you in a special time and place for His service?

Young Children: Draw a picture of Queen Esther standing before the king.

"WHO AM I" Game

There were a lot of main characters in the story of Esther. Let's play the "Who Am I?" game. A person will be described and you can guess who it is.

1. Esther was my younger cousin. Who am I?

____

2. I chose Esther to be the new queen. Who am I?

____

3. It was scary to enter the king's presence without being asked, but God provided me with the courage to do this. Who am I?

____

4. I wouldn't bow down and worship Haman. Only the one true God is to be worshipped. Who am I?

____

5. The king asked me how to honor someone. Who am I?

____

6. I was hung on the platform I built for Mordecai. Who am I?

____

7. God protected my life and the lives of my Jewish people. Who am I?

____

Episode 18

Job: Unanswered "Why's"

Do you have a habit of asking "Why?" Have you wondered why you didn't make the team or why your friend didn't invite you to the party? Or maybe you've questioned some life-changing events like why your parents got divorced or why a family member has cancer.

Job loved God and was a generous man, but when he experienced a lot of loss and personal pain, he began to ask, "Why?" Job learned that God doesn't always give us the answer. The real issue is, are we willing to trust God in spite of unanswered "whys?"

Now, use your imagination, as we journey back through time to look at the story, "Job: Unanswered 'Why's'."

(Story adapted from the book of Job)

My name is Job. I am excited to share with you how God worked in my life.

I lived in the land of Uz. I was an honest man and innocent of any wrong. At least that's the way I saw myself. I honored God and stayed away from evil. I had seven sons and three daughters. I owned seven thousand sheep, three thousand camels, five hundred pairs of oxen, and five hundred female donkeys. I had a large number of servants. I was the greatest man among all the people of the East.

God even said that no one on the earth was like me. But Satan questioned my motives. He believed that I trusted and obeyed God because my life was good. God had blessed me with a big family and lots of money. Satan said that if everything I had was destroyed, I would curse God. So God gave Satan permission to touch anything I had, but he couldn't touch me.

One day a messenger came and said the Sabians killed my servants and stole the oxen and cattle. While he was still speaking, another messenger said that lightning had burned up the sheep and the servants. While the second messenger was still speaking, another one said that the Babylonians stole all of the camels and killed the servants. The third messenger was still speaking when another man came to tell me that all of my sons and daughters were killed when the house collapsed on them.

I was so very sad, but I knew in my heart that God gave these things to me, and He took them away. I didn't understand why, but I bowed and worshipped God. I was naked when I was born, and I will be naked when I die. Praise the name of the Lord. In all this, I didn't blame God. I loved God for Who He was, not for what He gave me.

As if that wasn't enough, Satan wanted to attack my health. God agreed to let Satan touch my body, but not to the point of death. So Satan put painful sores all over my body, from the top of my head to the soles of my feet. I took a piece of broken pottery and used it to scrape my sores. My wife told me to curse God and die. I told her that she was talking foolishly. I asked her if we should take only good things from God and not trouble. In all this, I didn't sin in what I said.

Then my three friends, Eliphaz, Bildad, and Zophar came to see me. They sat on the ground with me for seven days and seven nights. No one said a word because they saw my pain. After seven days, I cursed the day I was born. Then, we went through several rounds of discussion about the reasons for my circumstances. In their effort to answer the "why" questions, my friends falsely accused me. I was frustrated with them, so I spoke directly to God. He still didn't answer my "whys," but He reminded me of Who He was—the Creator of the universe who spoke the world into being and created man out of dust. Nothing and no one can compare to God. He's all–powerful, all–knowing, and all–present. He loves you and He loves me unconditionally. It didn't matter to me anymore if God answered my "whys" because I knew I could trust Him—no matter what.

God not only restored my health, He gave me twice as much as I had owned before. I lived to see my children, grandchildren, great grandchildren, and great–great grandchildren. The Lord blessed the last part of my life even more than the first part.

Let's thank God for Who He is, that He is worthy of our trust. Pray these words of praise to Him:

God, thank You that You are all–powerful, all–knowing and all–present. You are everywhere at once. We can't understand that, but that's how great You are. Thank You that we can trust You in all of our circumstances, even when we don't have the answers to our "why" questions.

Use the book of Job and the Story to help you complete your Response. Then do the Activity.

Response

1. Job was the weakest man among all the people of the East.

   ❑ True ❑ False

2. Satan questioned Job's ____________________.

3. Job loved God for _______ _______ _________, not for what He ____________ ___.

4. In their effort to answer the "why" questions, Job's friends ____________________________ him.

   a. encouraged
   b. falsely accused
   c. blessed

5. It didn't matter to Job anymore if God answered his "whys" because he knew he could _______________ ___________—no matter what.

6. The Lord blessed the _______________ part of Job's life even more than the _______________ part.

7. Read this verse: "You asked, 'Who is this who hides counsel without knowledge?' Therefore I have uttered what I did not understand, things too wonderful for me, which I did not know" (Job 42:3).

Now write a letter to God or draw a picture about a time you thought you knew the answer to something, but then you realized that you didn't know the answer. Maybe it was something bigger than your understanding or experience. How did that make you feel? Example: I felt small compared to God.

Young Children: Draw a picture of some of the things that Job lost.

"Why" Questions

Instead of answering Job's "why" questions, God reminded Job of Who He was so Job knew he could trust God—no matter what.

Look at each of the character traits of God that are listed below. If you don't understand what some of them mean, put a checkmark beside them. Then, ask a grown-up to explain those character traits to you.

Character Traits of God

all-powerful	full of grace	just
unconditional love	kind	compassionate
all-knowing	merciful	not evil
truthful	patient	never fails
always present	holy	does not change
faithful	not limited by anything	the same yesterday, today and forever

God might not *change* your situation, but He will give you whatever you need to make it *through* the situation.

Episode 19

Daniel: Experiencing God in Hard Times

Have you ever been falsely accused of something because of your gifts and abilities? How did that make you feel?

Daniel was falsely accused of something because of his gifts and abilities. When the Babylonians took him captive, God gave him the ability to interpret dreams and reveal visions. This enabled him and his three friends to become top officials in the land.

Now, use your imagination, as we journey back through time to look at the story, "Daniel: Experiencing God in Hard Times."

Story

(Story adapted from the book of Daniel)

My name is Daniel. I am excited to share with you how God worked in my life.

Nebuchadnezzar, the king of Babylon, came to Jerusalem and captured our city with his army. I was one of several young Israelite men that he took back to Babylon to be trained to serve in his palace. He gave me the Babylonian name, Belteshazzar. My three friends were given the names Shadrach, Meshach, and Abed–nego. Because of my Jewish heritage, I did not want to eat the king's food and wine because it would make me ceremonially unclean. The person in charge agreed to let my three friends and me try our diet of vegetables and water for ten days. When he compared us to the others, we were healthier than all the other young men who ate the king's food.

Nebuchadnezzar had some dreams that bothered him so much he could not sleep. The fortunetellers, magicians, and wise men couldn't explain the dreams to him. They said that no one on the earth could do that! I told King Nebuchadnezzar that I could tell him what his dream meant—because God was with me. I asked my three friends to pray that God would reveal it to me. During the night, God explained the dream to me in a vision. I told the king that no man can do what he had asked, but the one, true God can explain secret things. I told him about God's Kingdom that will continue forever and never be destroyed. After I revealed the meaning of the dream, King Nebuchadnezzar fell face down on the ground and said, "God is the God of gods, the Lord of kings, and a revealer of secrets." The king put me in charge of all the wise men in Babylon.

Some time later, the king made a golden statue that stood ninety feet high and nine feet wide. He said that anyone who didn't bow down and worship the gold statue would be thrown into a fiery furnace. Shadrach, Meshach, and Abed–Nego did not bow down to the statue because they served the one, true God. Nebuchadnezzar became very angry, but he gave them another chance to worship the statue. They said they did not need to defend themselves because they believed God was able to save them from the fire. But even if God chose not to deliver them, they would rather die than bow down to the statue. Have you ever felt like you were being mistreated because you love God?

King Nebuchadnezzar was furious. He ordered the furnace to be heated seven times hotter than usual. The fire was so hot the flames killed the soldiers as they threw the three men into the furnace. Then Nebuchadnezzar said he saw four men walking around in the fire. They were not hurt, and the fourth man looked like the Son of God. Shadrach, Meshach, and Abed–Nego came out of the furnace. The fire had not harmed them at all.

Years later, Darius became the new king of Babylon. He planned to put me in charge of the whole kingdom. The other supervisors and governors were jealous, so they looked for a way to keep me from that position. They told the king to make a law that no one should pray to any god except to the king or be thrown into the lion's den. Have you ever felt like you were being persecuted for your faith? That's how I felt in this situation. The men found me on my knees praying to God just as I had always done. They threw me into the lion's den. The next morning, the king called out to me in the lion's den. He was glad when I answered and said that God sent His angel to close the mouths of the lions. I was not injured.

We don't always understand God's ways, but He is always seeking to reveal Himself to us. We can be sure that even when we experience challenges and hardship, God is always there.

Let's thank God that He is a revealer of secrets. Pray these words of praise to Him:

God, thank You that Your Kingdom will continue forever and never be destroyed. You are the God of gods, the Lord of kings. Thank You that I don't need to defend myself because I believe You are able to save me. Even if I am persecuted for my faith, You can send Your angel to "close the mouths of the lions." I don't always understand Your ways, but You are always seeking to reveal Yourself to me. I can be sure that even when I experience challenges and hardship, You are always there.

Use the book of Daniel and the Story to help you complete your Response. Then do the Activity.

1. Nebuchadnezzar, the king of Babylon, came to Jerusalem and celebrated with the city.

❑ True ❑ False

2. After Daniel revealed the meaning of the dream, King Nebuchadnezzar fell face down on the ground and said, ______________________

____

a. "Why me?"
b. "God is the God of gods, the Lord of kings, and a revealer of secrets."
c. "I won't repent."

3. Shadrach, Meshach, and Abed–Nego did not bow down to the statue because they served the ____________ ____________ ________________________.

4. King Darius was glad when Daniel answered and said that God sent His angel to ____________________ ____________ ____________________ ________ ____________ _________________.

5. We can be sure that even when we experience challenges and hardship, __________ __________________ ________________________ ________________________.

6. Read these verses: "I was watching in the night visions, and behold, One like the Son of Man, coming with the clouds of heaven! He came to the Ancient of Days, and they brought Him near before Him. Then to Him was given dominion and glory and a kingdom, that all peoples, nations, and languages should serve Him. His dominion is an everlasting dominion, which shall not pass away, and His kingdom the one which shall not be destroyed"
(Daniel 7:13–14).

Now draw a picture of Shadrach, Meshach, and Abed–Nego in the fiery furnace. Remember to show in your picture how God protected them with the fourth man.

Surrounded by Lions

Did you know?

- A lion is called "The King of the Beasts"
- An adult female lion eats 11 pounds of meat per day
- She weighs 260–330 pounds
- An adult male lion eats 15 pounds of meat per day
- He weighs 330–500 pounds

What else can you learn about lions? Write the facts below:

Try to imagine how Daniel felt when the lions surrounded him. Draw a picture of Daniel in the lion's den.

Episode 20

Jonah: No More Running

Have you ever tried to run from God because you had your own idea of the way you should go? How did things work out for you?

Jonah tried to run from God too. He had his own idea of the way he should go, and he took a ship to another city. Jonah tried to get away from God, but he couldn't.

Now, use your imagination, as we journey back through time to look at the story, "Jonah: No More Running."

(Story adapted from the book of Jonah)

My name is Jonah. I am excited to share with you how God worked in my life.

God said to go to the city of Nineveh and preach to them, for He saw their evil. Instead, I tried to run away from God. I found a ship that was going a different way, so I went on board. God sent a great wind, and the ship was in danger of breaking apart. The sailors began to throw cargo into the sea in order to make the ship lighter, so it wouldn't sink. They were afraid, so they cried out to their own god (which was not the real God). During this storm, I was asleep, but the captain woke me up and told me to call on my God to keep us from dying. The sailors asked me all kinds of questions about why this trouble had come upon them. I told them I was a Hebrew who worshiped God, the One who made the sea and the land, but that I was running away from Him.

The wind and the waves were getting stronger, so I told them to throw me into the sea, and then it would calm down. Instead, the sailors tried to row the ship back to the land. The wind and the waves were so strong they couldn't make it back to land. Have you ever reacted in your own strength against what God was doing? I told the sailors about my God, the One true God, and they called out to Him and believed in Him. Isn't it amazing how God uses difficult circumstances for His good?

Finally, they threw me into the sea, and it became perfectly calm. Then, God caused a great fish to swallow me. I was in the stomach of the fish for three days and three nights. I could barely get a breath of air. I thought I was locked in this prison forever, but God saved me from death. God spoke to the fish, and the fish vomited me out of its stomach onto the dry land.

God spoke to me again about going to Nineveh. This time I went. I preached to the people saying that after forty days the city would be destroyed. To my surprise, the people believed in God.

I was unhappy, however, that God did not destroy the city. I complained to Him because this is what I knew would happen. That's why I ran away. I knew He is a merciful and loving God, and He doesn't get angry quickly. He would rather forgive than harm.

I sat down outside of the city, and God made a plant grow up quickly over me. It provided shade for me. The next day, however, God sent a worm to attack the plant, and the plant died. Then, God sent a hot east wind, and I became weak from the heat. I was angry that the plant died. Then God showed me how wrong my thinking was. I showed more concern for a silly plant than for the people of Nineveh—more than one hundred and twenty thousand people lived in Nineveh. They needed to hear about God's love for them.

Looking back, I can see how personal God is. God wants to show me how much He loves me and cares for me in the middle of all the good, bad, and ugly things that happen to me. Despite my failure, God never gave up on me. In fact, He was always a step ahead of me! He wanted me to see His deep love for me, the sailors, and for all of the people of Nineveh. Being in the stomach of the fish for three days is a picture of God's Promised One, who would die for our sins, be buried for three days, and then rise from the dead to give new life to all who trust in Him. God truly cares for each person in all of the nations.

Let's thank God that He wants the best for us. Pray these words of praise to Him:

God, thank You that I don't have to run away from You. I don't have to react in my own strength against what You are doing. It's amazing how You use difficult circumstances for Your good. You are a merciful and loving God. You are a personal God, and You want to show me how much You love me and care for me in the middle of all the good, bad, and ugly things that happen to me. Despite my failure, You never give up on me. In fact, You are always a step ahead of me! You want me to see Your deep love for me. You truly care for each person in all of the nations.

Use the book of Jonah and the Story to help you complete your Response. Then do the Activity.

Response

1. God said to go to the city of Nineveh and preach to them, for He saw their good hearts.

❑ True ❑ False

2. Jonah told them he was a Hebrew who worshiped God, the One who made the sea and the land, but that he was ____________________ ________________ from Him.

3. Jonah told the sailors about his God, the One true God, and they called out to Him and ______________________ _____________ Him.

4. Despite Jonah's failure, God never gave up on him.

❑ True ❑ False

5. Being in the stomach of the fish for three days is a picture of God's ___________________ _________, who would die for our sins, be buried for three days, and then rise from the dead to give new life to all who trust in Him.

6. God truly ______________________________ each person in all of the nations.

a. bothers
b. cares for
c. spys on

7. Read this verse: "And he (Jonah) said: 'I cried out to the LORD because of my affliction, and He answered me'" (Jonah 2:2).

Now write a letter to God or draw a picture about a time you cried out to Him because you were hurting. Do you think He heard your cry? If so, did He give you an answer?

Young Children: Draw a picture of Jonah in the belly of the fish.

Timeline

Put these words from Jonah's story in the correct order on the list below.

storm	went to Nineveh	overboard	new life
swallowed by fish	ran away	preached to the people	ship

1.

2.

3.

4.

5.

6.

7.

8.

Episode 21

John the Baptist: Preparing the Way

Do you know what it means to be humble? We don't hear that word used very much today. It might be easier to understand if we know that being proud or arrogant is the opposite of being humble.

Humble is how John the Baptist felt when Jesus asked John to baptize Him. John was honored that Jesus would ask him, but he also felt humbled because of Who Jesus was, the long awaited Messiah. Jesus was so important that John didn't feel he could even tie the string of Jesus' sandals. But Jesus was never proud.

Now, use your imagination, as we journey back through time to look at the story, "John the Baptist: Preparing the Way."

(Story adapted from Matthew 3:1–17; Mark 1:1–12; Luke 1:5–80, 3:1–22; John 1:14–42, 3:22–36)

My name is John the Baptist. I am excited to share with you how God worked in my life.

During the time Herod ruled Judea, there was a priest named Zacharias and his wife's name was Elizabeth. They truly did what God said was good. They really wanted to have a baby, but both of them were very old so they had given up hope.

One day when it was Zacharias' turn to go into the temple and burn incense, an angel named Gabriel came and stood beside Zacharias. The angel told him not to be afraid. Gabriel said their prayers had been heard by God, and Elizabeth would give birth to a son. They were to name the baby John. Zacharias questioned Gabriel about how this could be true, but the angel told Zacharias that this baby boy was God's gift to them. He would be used by God in a special way. Then Gabriel told him some other surprising news. He said that Zacharias would not be able to talk until the baby was born, but he didn't say why.

There were many people outside praying while Zacharias was in the temple, and they were wondering why he was in there so long. Zacharias finally came outside, but he couldn't speak—

just as Gabriel said. Later, Elizabeth became pregnant—just as Gabriel said. Zacharias and Elizabeth were my parents.

During Elizabeth's sixth month of pregnancy, God sent the same angel, Gabriel, to a virgin named Mary. He said that she would become pregnant by the Holy Spirit and give birth to a son, and they were to name him Jesus. He would be called the Son of God. Soon after, Mary went to visit Elizabeth because they were relatives. Mary was very young and Elizabeth was very old, but both of them were surprised to be pregnant. Mary stayed with Elizabeth and helped her for about three months and then returned home.

When I was born, everyone assumed I would be named Zacharias because the firstborn son usually was named after his father. But my mother said that I would be named John. My father agreed, and as soon as my name was finalized, Zacharias could talk again. He began to praise God, and he told the people that I would be called a prophet of God. I would prepare the people for the coming of the Lord.

When I grew up, I began preaching in the desert area of Judah. I told people to change their lives and repent of their sin. Some of the Jews asked me if I was the Christ, the Messiah. I told them I was not the Christ, but I was the one Isaiah the prophet was talking about when he said, "I will send my messenger ahead of you. He will prepare your way. This is the voice of a man who calls out in the desert: 'Prepare the way for the Lord.'"

When they repented, I baptized them with water as a symbol to show that their hearts and lives had changed. But I always told them that when Jesus came, He was greater than I. In fact, He was so much greater, I didn't feel good enough to untie the strings of His sandals because Jesus was the Son of God.

Later, when I was baptizing some people in the Jordan River, I saw Jesus coming. I told them to look and see the Lamb of God who takes away the sins of the world. This is the One I was talking about. Then Jesus asked me to baptize Him. I was honored, but felt humble because of Who Jesus was, the Son of God. But I baptized Him, and when Jesus came up out of the water, God's Spirit came down from heaven and landed on Him like a dove. And a voice spoke from heaven and said, "This is my Son and I love Him. I am very pleased with Him."

Let's thank God for showing us how to be humble through John the Baptist and Jesus. Pray these words of praise to Him:

God, thank You that we can depend upon You to enable us to do anything we want to do. The Bible says we can do ALL things through Christ. Allow us to recognize when we act proud and let us remember to repent—turn the other direction—and recognize You as the Source of our success, not taking credit for ourselves.

Use Matthew 3:1–17; Mark 1:1–12; Luke 1:5–80, 3:1–22; John 1:14–42, 3:22–36 and the Story to help you complete your Response. Then do the Activity.

1. Zacharias and Elizabeth really wanted to have a baby, but both of them were very old.

❑ True ❑ False

2. Zacharias questioned Gabriel about how this could be true, but the angel told Zacharias that this baby boy was ____________ ____________ to them.

3. Zacharias began to praise God, and he told the people that John the Baptist would be called a __________________ ______ ______________.

4. John the Baptist would prepare the people for the coming of ________________________.
a. spring
b. new years
c. the Lord

5. Jesus was so much ____________________, John the Baptist didn't feel good enough to untie the strings of His sandals because Jesus was the _________________ _________ _________________.

6. Read this verse: "He must increase, but I must decrease" (John 3:30).

Now write a letter to God or draw a picture about a time you felt the "bigness" of God. Did you feel small in comparison? Did you feel humble and have the desire to "decrease?"

Young Children: Draw a picture of John the Baptist baptizing Jesus in the Jordan River.

Being Humble

Choose a word from the following list that belongs in the sentences that describe being humble.

FIRST • PRIDEFUL • ATTITUDE • OTHERS • GOD • ALL

H – Helping ____________________ be the best they can be—even if they become better than me.

U – Understanding that God can change a ________________________ attitude.

M – My actions think of others ________________.

B – Believing that in Christ, I can do _____________ things.

L – Living in dependence upon _____________.

E – Eliminating the need of acting arrogant in my _________________________.

Episode 22

Mary: Mother of Jesus

Have you ever had something totally unexpected happen in your life? How did you react?

Mary had something totally unexpected happen in her life. The angel Gabriel told her that she was going to become pregnant by the Holy Spirit, and that she would give birth to God's Son, the Promised One.

Now, use your imagination, as we journey back through time to look at the story, "Mary: Mother of Jesus."

(Story adapted from Matthew 1:18 to 2:23 and Luke 1:26 to 2:40)

My name is Mary. I am excited to share with you how God worked in my life.

I lived in Nazareth, a town in Galilee. I was engaged to marry a man named Joseph. God sent the angel Gabriel to tell me that I would become pregnant and give birth to a Son. I would name Him Jesus. He would be called the Son of the Most High. I asked the angel how this would happen since I was a virgin. The angel said that the Holy Spirit would be the father. Joseph didn't understand, so an angel of the Lord came to him in a dream. He told Joseph not to be afraid to take me as his wife because the baby in me was conceived by the Holy Spirit.

Joseph and I traveled to Bethlehem so our names would be listed as part of the family of David. While we were in Bethlehem the time came for our baby to be born. There were no rooms left in the inn, but the innkeeper said we could stay in the stable. When the baby was born, I wrapped Him in cloths and laid Him in a manger, the box where animals are fed. That night some shepherds were in the fields watching their sheep, and an angel of the Lord came to them. The glory of the Lord was shining around them, and suddenly they became very frightened. The angel said that he brought good news of great joy to all people, "Today your Savior is born in the city of David; He is Christ the Lord." Then a very large group of angels joined the first angel, and they were singing praises to God. The shepherds came to Bethlehem and told us what the angels had said about our newborn baby.

When baby Jesus was about 40 days old, we went to Jerusalem to present Him to God. In the temple, we met an elderly man named Simeon. The Holy Spirit told Simeon that he would not die before he saw the Promised One of God. When Simeon saw us, he took the baby in his arms and thanked God saying that his eyes had seen God's salvation, which God prepared before all people. Also, a prophetess named Anna was in the temple. She was eighty–four years old, and when she saw our baby, she began to thank God. And she talked about Jesus to all those who were waiting for the Messiah.

Down through the centuries, many people had been looking for and waiting on the Promised One. Jesus was the Promised One, the one who fulfilled that longing of the people for the Son of God who takes away the sins of the world. Have you been looking and waiting for Him? Have you been hoping for your chance to meet the Creator of the universe? Now you have that opportunity. Jesus came from heaven, became a baby, grew to be a man, died for our sins, rose again and returned to heaven. He conquered death so we could have eternal life. You can meet Him right now, right where you are.

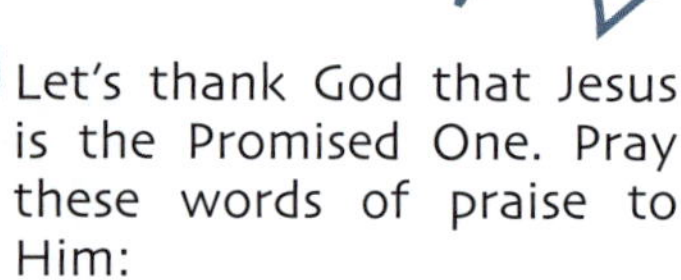

Let's thank God that Jesus is the Promised One. Pray these words of praise to Him:

God, thank You that You bring good news of great joy to me. Jesus, Your death on the cross was the payment for my sins, and Your resurrection gives me hope that I can live with You in Your kingdom forever. I want to meet You right now, right where I am.

Use Matthew 1:18 to 2:23, Luke 1:26 to 2:40, and the Story to help you complete your Response. Then do the Activity.

1. God sent the angel Gabriel to tell Mary that she would become pregnant and give birth to a Son.

   ❑ True ❑ False

2. When the baby was born, Mary wrapped Him in cloths and laid Him in a manger, the ______ ______________________________.

   a. decorated crib
   b. palace baby room
   c. box where animals are fed

3. That night some shepherds were in the fields watching their sheep, and ________________ ____________________ came to them.

   a. a wild animal
   b. an angel of the Lord
   c. King Herod

4. The glory of the Lord was shining around them, and suddenly they became very ____________.

   a. joyful
   b. frightened
   c. peaceful

5. Jesus was the ______________________ __________, the one who fulfilled that longing of the people for the Son of God who ____________ __________ ________ the sins of the world.

6. Read this verse: "And she [Mary] will bring forth a Son, and you shall call His name JESUS, for He will save His people from their sins" (Matthew 1:21).

Now draw a picture of your favorite part of the Christmas story, the night Jesus was born in a manger.

Word Scramble

Unscramble the following words that were used in today's story.

aeglns

arst

mropsied neo

raym

deehhprss

pesohj

sewi emn

ejssu

Episode 23

Jesus Christ: My Friend

God loves people. He promised to send the Promised One. The people wondered when this promise would be fulfilled. But God always keeps His promises.

God did not create Jesus Christ. Jesus has always been with God. He has no beginning or end. Jesus is God's Son. He came to earth as a human and showed people what God is like. He made a way for all people to be friends again with God.

Now, use your imagination, as we journey back through time to look at the story, "Jesus Christ: My Friend."

(Story adapted from the books of Matthew, Mark, Luke, and John)

This is Jesus Christ's story. He is telling the story as if He is talking to you.

God is Father, Spirit, and Son (Me). We have always lived together as one God. We have no beginning or end. We spoke the world into being, out of nothing. As part of Our forever plan, God the Father sent Me to rescue Our creation. Sin had made a gap between all people and God. I am the Promised One. I am the Bridge over the gap.

God the Spirit placed Me inside a young, unmarried girl named Mary. God is My Father. Mary became My mother as I lived on the earth in My physical body. Mary married a man named Joseph. Joseph became My earthly father. I was completely human and completely God—at the same time! Imagine creating something and then becoming one of your creations! I was born in the town of Bethlehem, and I grew up in the town of Nazareth. I had several sisters and brothers. I became a carpenter, just like My earthly father, Joseph.

When I was about thirty years old, I chose twelve "disciples," which means "learners." They were My closest friends. For three years, I taught My disciples and many other people about God's wonderful kingdom. I used stories to help the people understand. I healed people and raised people from the dead. I loved children and invited them to come to Me. I showed people what God is like.

Many people believed in Me, but the religious leaders thought the Promised One would be an earthly king. They wanted someone to save them from the evil kings and nations. They did not understand that the Promised One came to take away their sins and bring them close to God. They did not understand who I was or believe in Me. Instead, they wanted to kill Me. I wanted to bring them close to Me, but they did not want Me. That made Me very sad.

They arrested Me and put Me on trial for calling Myself God. Soldiers beat Me with a whip and made fun of Me. They made a crown out of thorns and pressed it into My head. I bled a lot. Then they nailed My hands and feet to a wooden cross and hung Me up to die. Only a few of My friends stayed with Me while I died. The others ran away or pretended not to know Me.

Satan, Our enemy, always comes to steal, kill, and destroy God's good things. I came to give people life to the full—the kind of life that Adam and Eve had in the Garden of Eden. But sin made a gap between all people and God, and no one measured up to God's requirements. The payment for sin is death. When the Israelites sinned, they sacrificed an animal. They had forgiveness—by faith through the Promised Lamb. I am the Promised Lamb—the Perfect Sacrifice for sins. I am the only One who measures up to God's perfect requirements. I never sinned, but I took the blame for everyone's sins—past, present, and future. I took on everyone's payment—death—and made things right between all people and God. It was horrible, but people were worth it.

Three days later, I came back to life so that people could live forever with Us and experience Our joy. I also appeared to My disciples several times. I told them that the Holy Spirit would come live in them. He would do My work through them. Then I went back to heaven. I hoped that people would want a friendship with God. I hoped that people would trust in Me instead of depending upon themselves.

I died for you because I love you. I died so that you could have forgiveness for sins once and for all. You are worth it. I came back to life so that you could live forever with Us and experience Our joy. Are you ready to trust in Me? Are you ready to admit that you can never be good enough on your own? Will you let Me give you My goodness? Will you accept My forgiveness—once and for all—for your sins? Will you let Me give you life to the full? It's a free gift. You can't earn it. Will you invite Me to live in you? God the Father wants you as His child. I want you as My sister or brother. We want to adopt you into Our forever family.

If you are ready to trust in Jesus instead of yourself, then pray these words to Him:

Jesus, I love You. Thank You for coming to earth. Thank You for dying for me and taking the blame for my sins. Thank You for coming back to life so that I could live with You forever. I know that I can never be good enough on my own. I want to trust in You instead of myself. Please come live inside me. I want to be God's adopted child.

Use the books of Matthew, Mark, Luke, John and the Story to help you complete your Response. Then do the Activity.

1. What made a gap between all people and God? ____________________

2. God sent Jesus Christ to be the Bridge over the gap and bring people close to God. Jesus is the Promised One.

❑ True ❑ False

3. Jesus is the only One who ______________ to God's perfect requirements. He was the Perfect Sacrifice for sins.

4. The payment for sin is ____________________.

5. Jesus never sinned; He (circle all the correct answers)
a. told others to try hard not to sin.
b. took the blame for everyone's sins — past, present, and future.
c. took on the payment—death—for everyone's sins.
d. said that we can be good enough on our own — if we do more good things than bad things.

6. Jesus came back to life so that ____________
____
____.

7. What do you think life to the full means?
____
____.
Can you be good enough to earn life to the full?

❑ Yes, I can earn it. ❑ No, it's a free gift.

8. How can you receive life to the full?
a. Admit that you can't be good enough on your own.
b. Trust in Jesus instead of yourself.
c. Accept Jesus' forgiveness—once and for all—for your sins.
d. Invite Jesus to live inside you.
e. All of the above

9. Read this verse: "For God so loved the world that He gave His only . . . Son, that whoever believes in Him should not perish [die] but have . . . life [forever]" (John 3:16).

Write a letter to God or draw a picture about what Jesus did for you.

Does Jesus live inside you? __________________

If so, when did you invite Him to live inside you?

❑ Today (write the date) _____________ ❑ A while back (write the date) _____________

Cross the Bridge

Sin made a gap between all people and God the Father. Solve the puzzle to find out how to cross the bridge, receive life to the full (forever!), and be adopted by God the Father.

Directions: The message below has "fallen" out of the puzzle. Each word of the message is in its correct column but not in the correct order. Put the words back into the grid and rebuild the message, one word per box. The first two words have been done for you.

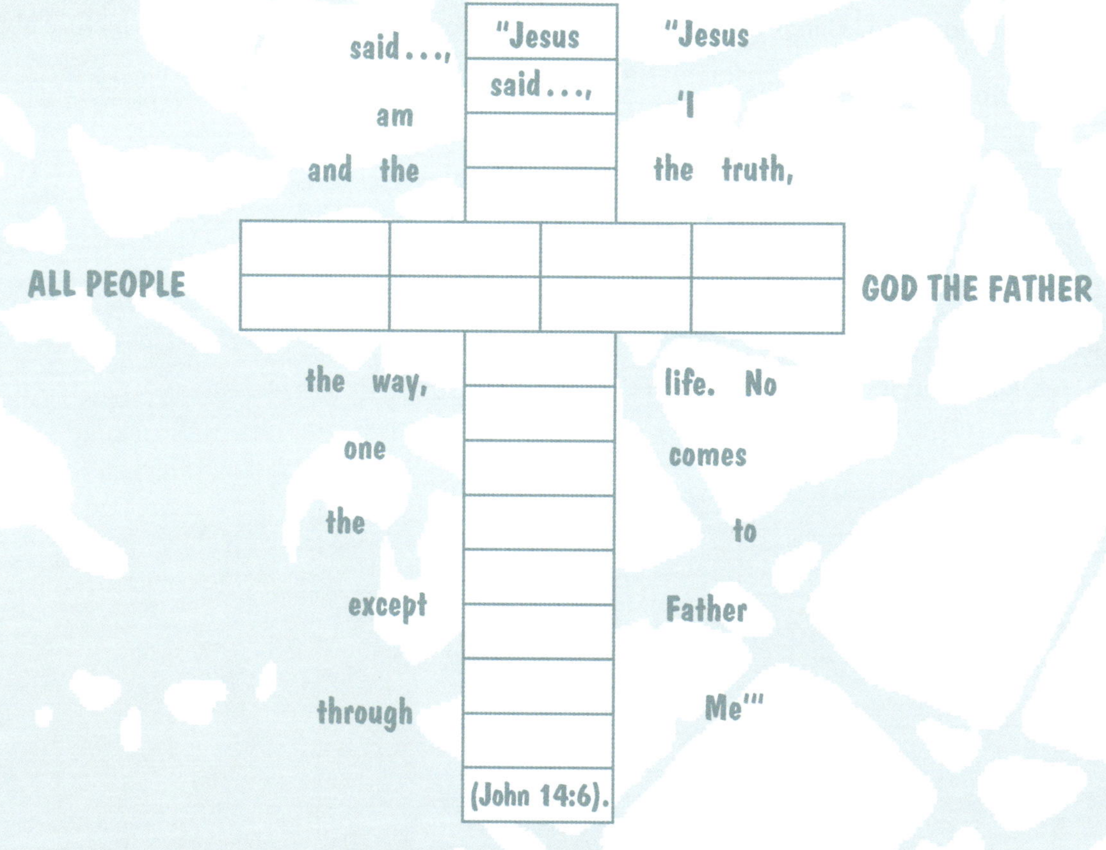

______________ is the Promised One. ______________ is the Bridge over the gap.

Episode 24

Peter: Peer Pressure

Have you ever gone along with the crowd because you didn't want to be different? You didn't choose to act like a child of God because you were too afraid. Did you think that you had the courage to respond one way, but you did just the opposite? What happened?

Peter understands. He was sure that he would always be a bold witness for Jesus. He even told Jesus that he would die for Him. But at one point, Peter discovered it was easier to blend into the crowd than to admit he knew Jesus.

Now, use your imagination, as we journey back through time to look at the story, "Peter: Peer Pressure."

Story

(Story adapted from the New Testament books written by Peter and the Gospels, specifically Matthew 26:31–35, 69–75; Mark 14:27–31, 66–72; Luke 22:31–34, 54–62; John 18:15–27, 21:1–23)

My name is Peter. I am excited to share with you how God worked in my life.

I was invited by Jesus to travel with Him and eleven other disciples for three years while He ministered on earth. I had so many experiences in those three years, but I'll only be able to tell you a few of the stories in this episode. There are a lot more that you can read about in the Bible.

Just before Jesus went back to heaven, He told all of us disciples that we would lose our faith. I told Him that all the others may lose their faith, but I never would. Jesus told me that on that very night I would say I didn't know Him three different times before a rooster crowed. I argued that I would never say I didn't know Him. I said that I would even die for Him. Soon after this conversation, Jesus was arrested and taken away.

That evening, a servant girl recognized me as one of Jesus' disciples. I denied that I knew Him and left the courtyard. At the entrance of the gate, one of the servants saw me and asked if I had been with Jesus in the garden. Again I said that I wasn't with Him. A short time later, some people said that they knew I was one of the men that followed Jesus. I swore that I didn't know Him. As soon as I denied knowing Jesus the third time, a rooster crowed. Then Jesus turned and looked straight at me. I remembered that He told me I would deny Him three times before a rooster crowed. I was so sorry. I went outside and cried. I was disappointed in my actions. I thought I would have the courage to die for what I believed about Jesus, but instead I did just the opposite. Throughout the rest of my life, Jesus gave me many chances to be identified as one of His followers, and I realized it was His courage in me (not my own courage) that made me be a bold witness for Him.

After Jesus' crucifixion and resurrection, we were on Lake Galilee fishing. We fished all night but caught nothing. Early the next morning, a man standing on the shore asked us if we had caught any fish. We said no. He told us to throw our net onto the right–hand side of the boat, and we would catch some fish. We did this and caught so many fish that we could not pull the net back into the boat. Then I realized the man on the shore was Jesus. I jumped into the water to swim to meet Him. The others went to the shore in the boat, dragging the net full of fish. On the shore, Jesus was cooking breakfast for us. After we ate, Jesus asked me three times in three different ways if I loved Him. Each time I answered, "Yes, I love You." By the third time I said, "Lord, You know all things; You know that I love You."

After each time He asked if I loved Him, Jesus told me to feed His sheep. It's one thing to say you love Jesus, but it's another thing to allow Him to serve others through you. That day was a turning point for me; I knew I was forgiven. Jesus gave me the chance to commit my love and my life to Him three times—the same number of times I denied Him. Then He said, "Follow Me." I didn't know where the future would lead, but I knew I could trust Jesus no matter what happened. By the end of my life, I did have the courage to die for Jesus. I asked to be crucified upside down because I didn't want to die the same way my Lord died. I'm living proof that Jesus has forgiven you, and He will give you the courage to be all that He wants you to be.

Let's thank God that He can give us the courage not to follow the crowd and allow us to do what He wants, so that others may see His love.

God, thank You that I don't have to be afraid to be different from the crowd. I can trust You to enable me to act like a child of God when I feel like doing the opposite. Thank You that You have already forgiven me when I mess up just like you did with Peter. I want others to see my love for You. I am willing to live my life in serving others to see them come to know of Your free gift of eternal life.

Use Matthew 26:31–35, 69–75; Mark 14:27–31, 66–72; Luke 22:31–34, 54–62; John 18:15–27, 21:1–23 and the Story to help you complete your Response. Then do the Activity.

1. Peter was invited by Jesus to travel with Him and eleven other disciples for three years while He ministered on earth.

❏ True ❏ False

2. Jesus told Peter that on that very night he would say he didn't know Him three different times before ______________________________.

a. Big Ben struck 12 o'clock midnight
b. a rooster crowed
c. Cinderella's carriage turned into a pumpkin

3. Peter thought he would have the courage to ____________________ for what he believed about Jesus, but instead he did just the opposite.
a. dance
b. sing
c. die

4. Then Peter realized the man on the shore was ________________________.
a. Jesus
b. Moses
c. John the Baptist

5. It's one thing to say you love Jesus, but it's another thing to allow Him to __________ ____________________________ through you.

6. Peter didn't know where the future would lead, but he knew he could ________________ Jesus no matter what happened.

7. Peter is living proof that Jesus has __________________ you, and He will give you the ________________________ to be all that He wants you to be.

8. Read this verse: "And the Lord turned and looked at Peter. Then Peter remembered the word of the Lord, how He had said to him, 'Before the rooster crows, you will deny Me three times'" (Luke 22:61).

Now write a letter to God or draw a picture about a time you felt you denied the Lord. Did you sense His forgiving and loving gaze upon you? Think about what you learned from that experience. For example, one thing you might have learned is that you can do nothing in your own strength. But in God's strength, you can do amazing things.

Young Children: Draw a picture of Peter and the rooster crowing.

FEED MY SHEEP

Peter was known for being "impulsive." He often acted before he thought. When he recognized that it was Jesus on the shore cooking breakfast, Peter jumped into the water to swim to Jesus. He didn't even think about it for a minute. Unscramble the following words that describe what we learned about Peter and Jesus in today's episode.

1. Jesus told Peter that he would deny Him three times in one night before the *(SOORETR)* ______________________ crowed.

2. Peter was (PLUMIVESI) ____________________ all three times he denied knowing Jesus. He was so disappointed in his actions that he went outside and *(DRICE)*_______________.

3. Peter *(PUMEJD)* _______________ into the water to swim to Jesus on the shore.

4. Jesus had already *(NGRIFEVO)* ____________ Peter for denying Him and told Peter to feed His *(PEHESI)* ____________.

5. Peter is *(GLINIV FOROP)* _____________ _______ that Jesus can give us the courage to be all that He wants us to be.

Episode 25

Peter: Learn From Failure

Have you ever felt left out of a group? Maybe your family moved to a new town and you didn't know anybody. You felt like an outsider in your classroom. Or have you watched certain people get "special treatment" because they have money or a lot of influence?

We learn from today's episode, that Jesus treats everybody the same way. He loves and accepts all people, regardless of where they come from.

Now, use your imagination, as we journey back through time to look at the story, "Peter: Learn from Failure."

(Story adapted from the New Testament books written by Peter, the Gospels, and specifically Acts 2:1–42, 3:1–22, 10:1–48)

My name is Peter. I am excited to share with you how God worked in my life.

Jesus promised us that after His departure He would send the Holy Spirit to be our Helper. We didn't know exactly what that meant, but here's how it happened. One day when I was preaching, a most unusual thing happened. While I was telling everyone about the great things God had done, Jesus poured out His Spirit on us. People started speaking in their own native tongue, but everybody understood everybody else! I said if they believed in Jesus, they would receive the gift of the Holy Spirit and have a new heart. That day about 3000 people were added to the number of believers. That event was called the Day of Pentecost, the birth of God's Church. The word "pentecost" means "fiftieth day." Some churches still celebrate Pentecost Sunday—50 days following Easter.

On our way to the Temple one day, John and I walked by a man who had been crippled all his life. Every day he begged for money outside the Temple. When he asked us for money, we told him that we didn't have any silver or gold, but we could give him something better. I lifted the man up by his right hand and by the power of Jesus Christ, he immediately began walking, jumping, and praising God. All of the people recognized him as the crippled beggar. They were amazed and couldn't understand how this happened. They looked at us like it was our own power that made the man walk, but we told them it was by the power of Jesus that he was completely well. We were warned not to talk to people anymore about Jesus, but we said that we could not be quiet. We would obey God rather than men.

At Caesarea there was a man named Cornelius, an officer in the Roman Army. He and his family were Gentiles, but they worshipped the true God. One afternoon, Cornelius saw a vision of an angel who told him to send some men to Joppa and bring me back to him. Cornelius obeyed the angel.

I was going up on the roof to pray (that was my custom), and I had a vision. I saw heaven open and something that looked like a big sheet was lowered to the earth by its four corners. In it were all kinds of animals, reptiles, and birds. Then a voice said for me to get up, kill and eat. I was hungry and wanted to eat, but I said, "no," because I had never eaten food that was unholy and unclean. Jewish people were only supposed to eat certain things according to the Jewish Law. But the voice told me that God had made these things clean. This happened three times and then the sheet with all of the animals disappeared.

While I was wondering what the vision meant, Cornelius' men found my house. The Spirit told me to go with them. When we arrived in Caesarea, Cornelius was waiting for us. It was against our Jewish law for me (a Jew) to associate with anyone who was not a Jew. But God showed me that I shouldn't call Gentiles unholy or unclean. Every person is the same to God, regardless of his nationality. I told the group that everyone who believes in Jesus will be saved. While I was still speaking, the Holy Spirit came down on all those who were listening. It was the first time that the Jewish believers realized that the gift of the Holy Spirit was also given to non-Jewish people. It was an amazing day.

Let's thank God that He doesn't show any partiality. Everyone who believes in Jesus will be saved regardless of what country he's from.

God, thank You for sending the Holy Spirit to be our Helper. And thank You that He comes to all who believe—to Jewish people and Gentiles. It is through His power that our hearts can become new. Work through us so that we can accept all people. Thank You Jesus that You died for everyone.

Use Acts 2:1–42, 3:1–22, 10:1–48 and the Story to help you complete your Response. Then do the Activity.

Response

1. Jesus promised us that after His departure He would send the Holy Spirit to be our Helper.

❑ True ❑ False

2. When the beggar asked Peter and John for money, they told him that they didn't have any ______________ ______ ____________, but they could give him something ______________.

3. The people looked at Peter and John like it was their own power that made the man walk, but Peter and John told them it was by the power of ______________ that he was completely well.

a. meditation
b. positive thinking
c. Jesus

4. Peter and John would obey _______________ rather than _____________.

5. God loves every person equally, regardless of his nationality, hair style, personality, or education.

❏ True ❏ False

6. Peter told the group that everyone who believes in ___________________ will be __________________.

7. Read these verses: "Then Peter opened his mouth and said: 'In truth I perceive that God shows no partiality. But in every nation whoever fears Him and works righteousness is accepted by Him'" (Acts 10:34–35).

Now write a letter to God or draw a picture about why you believe you are accepted by Him.

Young Children: Draw a picture of Peter's vision of a big sheet with all kinds of animals, reptiles, and birds in it.

NO PARTIALITY

Directions: Start at the arrow, and follow the letters until you reach the period.

Y	T	H	E	Y	A	R	E.
	A					J	
		W			E		
		E		S			
	H		U				
T		S					
T	A	C	C	E	P	T	S
S							A
U							L
J	E	L	P	O	E	P	L

Write the phrase on the lines below.

____

____

Episode 26

Paul: Light From Heaven

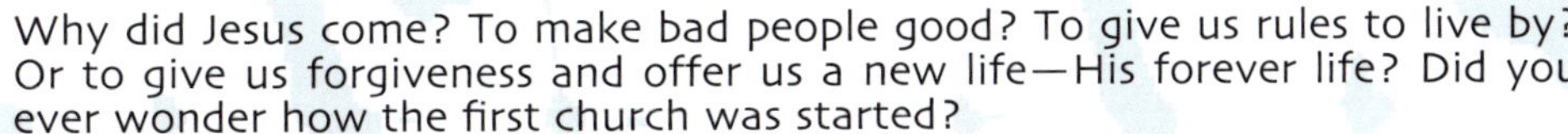

Why did Jesus come? To make bad people good? To give us rules to live by? Or to give us forgiveness and offer us a new life—His forever life? Did you ever wonder how the first church was started?

When Jesus went back to heaven, He promised His disciples to send the Holy Spirit to live within them. Jesus' disciples would share the good news of His forgiveness and teach new believers to depend upon Him.

About ten days later, the Holy Spirit came into the believers, just as Jesus had promised. Those new believers were so excited, they told anyone who would listen about Jesus. Many trusted in Jesus, and that's how the first church began. Later, a man named Paul helped take the good news about Jesus to Europe.

Now, use your imagination, as we journey back through time to look at the story, "Paul: Light from Heaven."

Story

(Story adapted from the New Testament books written by the Apostle Paul, the Gospels, and specifically Acts 8:1–3, 9:1–25)

My name is Paul. I am excited to share with you how God worked in my life.

When I first met Jesus, my name was Saul. I was one of the religious leaders called a Pharisee. I didn't understand that Jesus was God's Son, so I put His believers in jail and tried to destroy all of the Christians. I thought Jesus and His followers were trying to destroy God's name. I didn't realize that Jesus was the Messiah, the Promised One of God.

The religious leaders even gave me permission to find and arrest believers in the city of Damascus. On my way to Damascus, a bright light from heaven flashed around me. When I fell to the ground, I heard a voice call my name, "Saul! Why are you doing things against Me?" It was Jesus. He told me to get up and go into the city. The light had blinded me! My friends had to lead me into Damascus.

At the same time, God spoke to a believer named Ananias who lived in Damascus. Ananias found me and explained that Jesus had sent him to help me. When he laid his hands on my eyes, something like fish scales fell from my eyes. I could see! I stayed in Damascus for a few days.

Then I began to tell people about Jesus, the Son of God. Everyone was surprised because they knew I had spent most of my time trying to destroy the early Church. Now the Holy Spirit filled me with the desire to prove that Jesus is God's Son. I was a new person from the inside out. I was no longer Saul who tried to destroy Christians. Now I was Paul who believed that Jesus was the Messiah, the Promised One. The Jews in Damascus could not argue with me, so they plotted to kill me. Some friends helped me get out of town.

Jesus taught me His truth. I traveled around many cities and taught people the truth about Him. I got to watch churches start. I wrote letters to the churches and to my friends. Some of my letters are in the Bible—God's love letter to all people.

I loved to speak about Jesus and let Him live through me. God wants to make peace with all people. It's His gift. When we reject Jesus we reject the life He wants to give us forever. God sent Jesus to show us what God's love is like. God's love is incredible! Jesus made the way for us to be friends with God again, and not just friends but His children. God gives us a new life through Jesus, His Son.

Have you trusted in Jesus Christ and accepted God's forgiveness for your sins? Have you received new life in Christ and begun your journey with Him? If so, wonderful! You will learn more about that journey in the episodes that follow.

If not, you can know the Creator of the universe. Jesus Christ came to die to forgive our sins. Then He rose from death to new life. When we accept God's forgiveness, Jesus gives us a new life, His forever life. He wants to live through you and be your forever friend.

If you have never trusted in Jesus, then you can pray these words to Him:

Jesus, thank You for loving me. Thank You for dying and taking the blame for my sins. I accept Your forgiveness. I know that I can never be good enough on my own. Please come live inside me and through me. Please give me Your new life.

Use Acts 8:1–3, 9:1–25 and the Story to help you complete your Response. Then do the Activity.

1. Saul didn't understand that Jesus was God's Son, so he put His believers in jail and tried to destroy all of the Christians.

❑ True ❑ False

2. On Saul's way to Damascus, a bright ____________ from heaven flashed around him.

a. lightning bolt
b. light
c. fire

3. When Saul fell to the ground, he heard a voice call his name, "Saul! Why are you doing things against Me?" It was ____________________________.

4. After his experience on the Damascus Road, Saul the persecuter became Paul, the one who preached. Now the Holy Spirit filled Paul with the desire to prove that Jesus is _____________ _____________.

5. Some of Paul's letters are in the Bible—God's _______________ _________________ to all people.
a. iron hammer
b. loud megaphone
c. love letter

6. God wants to make peace with ________ people.
a. some
b. many
c. all

7. Read this verse: "As he [Saul] journeyed he came near Damascus, and suddenly a light shone around him from heaven" (Acts 9:3).

Saul was persecuting (hurting) Christians when God got his attention with a bright light on the Damascus Road. Saul became a new person that day. He not only stopped hurting Christians, he became a Christian. Paul spent the rest of his days on earth allowing Jesus to live His forever life in Him.

Now write a letter to God or draw a picture about a time God did something special in your life. What would happen if you allowed Jesus to live His forever life in you? What if you allowed Jesus to love your parents, your friends, and even your enemies through you?

Young Children: Draw a picture of Saul and the bright light coming down from heaven.

Jesus Is the Light

The puzzle below is from Acts 9:3 and Romans 5:8–10. Find and circle the following words hidden in the puzzle. The words may be forward, backward, horizontal, vertical, or diagonal.

DAMASCUS	LOVE
HEAVEN	NEW
JOURNEY	RECONCILED
LIFE	RIGHTEOUS
LIGHT	SINNER

```
D N H H X L K E K R U S S Z H
L E W E I C K A S G M U I O Y
Y N L G A N E U E I L O N B W
Z T H I A V C E F I L E N R P
W T W O C S E B U W Y T E P X
N K E R A N A N T U Z H R T R
B H O M I B O V R Y O G M R Q
X E A L U G Z C O S W I G Q D
C D V J O U R N E Y J R Z Z Z
W O S O Y X U W B R W F A W Q
K A Q X L K Y P B U J T O E V
V P O P O N T P K A I Q Y N K
I I Y M C G X T A S C Q O X M
C O T H N U T Q T O J I J W D
B I R V V U J Y M E L I S M R
```

Episode 27

Paul: Receiving the Light

Why did God make people? Why are we here? We were made to be loved by God and to spread His love to others.

Do most people experience God's love in this way every day? No! What prevents us from experiencing His love and allowing it to impact others? We do. We try to force ourselves to love God and be nice to our friends. It's impossible! Love only comes from God. Jesus died for us, so He could live through us. This is good news!

Now, use your imagination, as we journey back through time to look at the story, "Paul: Receiving the Light."

Story

(Story adapted from the New Testament books written by the Apostle Paul, the Gospels, and specifically Acts 9:26–30, 11:19–30, 12:25 to 15:35)

My name is Paul. I helped take the good news about Jesus to Europe. Many people believed in Jesus, and I wrote letters to the churches and to my friends. You can read more about my adventures in the New Testament.

After I left Damascus, I went back to Jerusalem. I tried to join Jesus' friends, but they were afraid of me. After all, I had tried to arrest them before I believed in Jesus. One man, named Barnabas, accepted me and took me to the church leaders. Barnabas told them that I had heard the Lord on the road to Damascus and had seen His light. It had even blinded me for a while! Barnabas could tell that Jesus now lived in me because I talked about Jesus so boldly in Damascus. So Barnabas convinced Jesus' friends that Jesus lived through me, and I stayed with them. I told people the good news about Jesus all over Jerusalem.

Before I knew Jesus, I was not a good person. I tried to do good things. Remember, I was a leader in my religion. But no matter how hard I tried, I could not be good. Only God is good. Only Jesus living in me makes me good. The Spirit of God changed me and gave me a new life. He gave me love, joy, peace, patience, kindness, goodness, faithfulness, gentleness, and self–control. When Jesus came to live inside me, I no longer wanted to do evil things.

In Jerusalem, some people wanted to kill me because they didn't like what I was preaching. So my friends helped me get to the city of Tarsus—my hometown. Then Barnabas, my good friend, came, and we went to the city of Antioch.

The church in Antioch sent Barnabas and me out to travel the world and share the good news of Jesus—that's what a missionary does. We were some of the first missionaries to tell the Jews about Jesus. Some people believed. Some argued against us. Then the Lord told us to go to non-Jews. Many people believed, and the message of the good news spread rapidly.

I met a crippled man who had never walked. The man had faith that God could heal him. I told him to stand up on his feet. The man jumped up and walked. The crowd was so impressed they shouted and claimed that we were like some of their gods. (They worshipped all kinds of non-human idols.) We told them we were only human beings like them, but we had put our faith in the living God, and they were seeing His power, not ours. God did many wonderful things through us. He did it, not us.

Some people didn't like what I was saying and they threw big stones at me—so many, they thought I was dead. Then they dragged me out of the town. But God wanted me to keep telling people about His Son, Jesus, so He didn't let me die that day. In fact, God gave me the strength the next day to leave with Barnabas and go to another city.

When I was younger and did not know Jesus, I only trusted in myself and I was very proud. I did all of the right things. I lived by the Law of Moses and kept all of the rules. I was a religious leader, but I tried to hurt the Church because I didn't know about Jesus. I just knew about the man-made rules of my religion, but now I know that keeping the rules of my religion didn't give me peace with God. My right standing with God doesn't come from following religious laws; it comes from trusting in Jesus. He can meet all of my needs—no matter what happens.

I just want to know God as much as possible. I want His life and His power to live through me. When we trust in Jesus, we have a treasure in us—the Holy Spirit—but we are like clay jars and they can break easily. When I am broken, it means I realize that I cannot save myself or anyone else from anything. Being broken is the opposite of being proud. Only then can I have confidence in God. When God does incredible things through our lives, it proves that the power is from God, not from us!

Let's thank God for His great power that works through us. Pray these words of praise to Him:

God, thank You that You can change me and give me a new life. I want to let Christ live through me. This will prove that the power is from God, not from me.

Use Acts 9:26-30, 11:19-30, 12:25 to 15:35 and the Story to help you complete your Response. Then do the Activity.

1. Barnabas accepted Paul and took him to the church leaders.

   ❑ True ❑ False

2. When Jesus came to live inside Paul, he no longer wanted to do ____________ things.

3. The Lord told Paul and Barnabas to go to ______________________ and tell them about the new life in Jesus.

4. The crowd was so impressed they shouted and claimed that Paul and Barnabas were like some of their gods. (The people worshipped all kinds of non–human idols.) Paul and Barnabas told them that they were only ______________ ______________ like them, but Paul and Barnabas had put their faith in the living God, and they were seeing His power, not theirs.
a. insecure people
b. religiously superstitious
c. human beings

5. Our right standing with God doesn't come from following __________ __________; it comes from trusting in Jesus.

6. When we trust in Jesus, we have a treasure in us—__________ ______________— but we are like ____________________ ______________ and they can break easily. When God does incredible things through our lives, it proves that the power is from God, not from us!

7. Read this verse: "[Paul was] strengthening the souls of the disciples, exhorting them to continue in the faith, and saying, 'We must through many tribulations enter the kingdom of God'" (Acts 14:22).

Now write a letter to God or draw a picture about a time you had to go through tribulations. (Tribulations means troubles.)

Young Children: Draw a picture of Paul and Barnabas preaching.

Live your Destiny

Jesus Christ expressing Himself through us gives God His highest glory. Glory means the highest expression of something or someone. A ballerina's highest expression would be her most beautiful dance. God's greatest glory is Jesus. Jesus is the source of love and life. Christ in me, the hope of glory means that it is only with Christ in me that I can be who I was created to be.

When we try to meet our needs without Jesus, the Bible calls this sin or "flesh" and it leads to death—the opposite of the life we have with Jesus. As believers, sin or flesh no longer has power over us, but we can choose to give in to our temptations.

The power of sin is like a splinter in our finger. The small fragment of wood is not us, but it's in us. Just because we have a splinter in our finger doesn't mean we are a solid piece of wood—like a wooden baseball bat! That's not who we are. When we walk after our flesh, it hinders God's expression of Christ through us. Are you ready to live like who God created you to be? Are you ready to put your confidence in God instead of yourself? (See Philippians 3:3)

List the words that belong under the Jesus column and the flesh column.

	Jesus as the Source	Flesh as the Source
joy idolatry witchcraft patience envy gentleness peace kindness drunkenness hate troublemaking self–control purity		

If you have placed your faith in Jesus, you have everything in the Jesus column—joy, patience, gentleness, peace, kindness, self–control, and purity. In Christ you are a new creation. And because He lives in you, you are no longer a slave to sin. Being controlled by things in the flesh column like hate or witchcraft, is no longer who you are. You are who you are because of Whose you are. Now, let Jesus shine His love to those around you! (See Philippians 3:9 and 2 Corinthians 4:7.)

Episode 28

Paul: Reflecting the Light

Who are you? Are you an athlete, student, or musician? No, that is just a description of what you may do. You are who you are because of whose you are, not because of what you do. Who do you belong to? No matter how you behave, if you belong to Jesus, you are a saint. If you belong to the world, you are a sinner.

The truth is, a child of God has great power. Jesus is our source of power. When we live like children of God, people see His light and confidence in us. This is the way we get to participate with God in bringing the good news to people everywhere. He made us holy, and we can trust His holiness and glory to shine through us. It's an impossible life to live on our own.

Now, use your imagination, as we journey back through time to look at the story, "Paul: Reflecting the Light."

Story

(Story adapted from the New Testament books written by the Apostle Paul, the Gospels, and specifically Acts 16:16 to 17:34)

My name is Paul. I want to share another story of how God worked in the life of a jailer and his family.

On one of my journeys with my friend, Silas, we met a slave girl with an evil spirit. She told fortunes and earned a lot of money for her owner. She kept following us and calling out to us. The evil spirit in her knew who we were and that we were telling people about Jesus. Finally, I commanded the spirit to come out of her. It did. But the owner didn't like it, because now she couldn't tell fortunes anymore, and she wasn't earning any money for him. We were dragged into the market place and accused of causing trouble. We were beaten and thrown into jail. The officials told the jailer to make sure we didn't escape. The jailer put us in the most secure cell he had.

At midnight, a big earthquake broke open the doors of the jail. When the jailer woke up and saw the jail doors open, he thought that we had escaped. He began to kill himself with his own sword, because he knew his boss would kill him if we had escaped. I shouted to him, "Don't hurt yourself! We are all here!"

The jailer could not believe his eyes. He ran into our cell and fell down before us, shaking with fear. He asked us what he must do to be saved. We told him the great news about the Lord Jesus. I explained that all he needed to do was believe and trust in Jesus, and he and his family would be saved.

To help the jailer, I had to know who I was—my true identity as a child of God with all of Christ's power inside of me. Apparently, the jailer saw my confidence, and God worked through me. The jailer and his whole family put their trust in Jesus that very night.

Later we went to Athens. The city was full of statues that the people worshipped. They called these statues "gods." Some of the people had never heard of the one true God, so I talked with many Jews and Greeks in the synagogue and the marketplace and told them the story of how God the Father sent His Son Jesus to the earth.

Jesus is the reason we can have peace with God. We can only have peace with God by trusting in Jesus. When we trust in Jesus, He takes our old life and gives us His new life. Jesus is God's Son and when we trust in Him we become part of God's family—we are God's children, we become one with Him. We have a union with God the Father and with Jesus that cannot be broken.

Let's thank God that we can trust Him when we feel afraid. Pray these words of praise to Him:

Dear God, as a believer in You I know who I am—I am Yours. I'm a child of God with all of Christ's power inside of me. I am one with You. Thank You that our union cannot be broken.

Use Acts 16:16 to 17:34 and the Story to help you complete your Response. Then do the Activity.

1. On one of Paul's journeys with his friend, Silas, they met a slave girl with an evil spirit. She told fortunes and earned a lot of money for her owner. She kept following them and helping them.

❑ True ❑ False

2. The jailer could not believe his eyes. He ran into Paul and Silas' cell and fell down before them,

____.

He asked them what he must do to be ______________________.

3. To help the jailer, Paul had to know who he was—

____

____.

a. a missionary
b. a former Pharisee
c. his true identity as a child of God with all of Christ's power inside of him

4. The city was full of statues that the people ____.

5. ______________________ is the reason we can have peace with God.

a. Statues of other gods
b. Jesus
c. Paul

6. When we trust in Jesus, He takes our ______________ ______________ and gives us His ______________ ______________. Jesus is God's Son and when we trust in Him we become part of ______________ ________________________—we are God's children, we become ______________ with Him. We have a ______________________ with God the Father and with Jesus that cannot be broken.

7. Read this verse: "For in Him we live and move and have our being" (Acts 17:28).

Have you ever had an experience that could have only been God? What was it like? Now write a letter to God or draw a picture about a time you knew God was working through your life. Is there something you are afraid of? Put that in your letter or picture as well. Don't allow fear to imprison you. God can set you free, just like He did Paul.

Young Children: Draw a picture of the jail after the earthquake.

CHRIST IN YOU

1. Take a cup.
– This represents your body.

2. Add a drink powder mix in the cup.
– The drink powder mix represents your soul and the color represents your personality.

3. Pour water into the cup and stir it together with the drink powder mix.
– The water represents the Spirit of God who comes into your life when you place your trust in Jesus Christ.

The water dissolves the drink powder mix, and it becomes something new. It blends totally with the water and becomes one substance with the water. This is how your life in Christ is. The water didn't change the color and flavor of your personality.

Read the three truths below, and write them on the drawing of the cup. Use a pen. Then color the cup lightly. The next time you feel discouraged, look at the cup. It will remind you of God's truth about you.

In Christ I am:

- holy
- righteous
- valuable and accepted

I am all of these, not because of anything I can do. I am holy, righteous, and valuable and accepted because I am God's child and Jesus lives in me. (See Ephesians 4:24 and Matthew 10:31.)

Episode 29

Paul: Trusting the Light

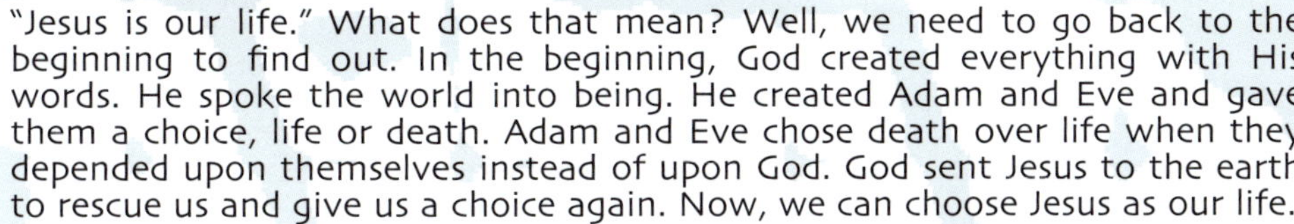

"Jesus is our life." What does that mean? Well, we need to go back to the beginning to find out. In the beginning, God created everything with His words. He spoke the world into being. He created Adam and Eve and gave them a choice, life or death. Adam and Eve chose death over life when they depended upon themselves instead of upon God. God sent Jesus to the earth to rescue us and give us a choice again. Now, we can choose Jesus as our life.

Jesus died to pay for our sins—past, present, and future. The Bible says when He walked on earth Jesus was tempted in every way like we are, but He did not sin. He was perfect, so God could accept His death as payment for our sins.

When Jesus rose again, He broke the power of sin. Remember the splinter illustration in an earlier story? The person who trusts in Jesus identifies with His death and resurrection (resurrection means rising from the dead). Our identity is who we are. When we identify with Jesus, we understand that our old sinner person died with Him, was buried with Him, and we are resurrected with Him in new life. Jesus now lives His life through us.

Now, use your imagination, as we journey back through time to look at the story, "Paul: Trusting the Light."

Story

(Story adapted from the New Testament books written by the Apostle Paul, the Gospels, and specifically Acts 19:23 to 21:14)

My name is Paul. As I continued to preach about Jesus, some people wanted to hurt me, but others chose to believe in Jesus. They encouraged me and prayed for me.

In one particular city, I met a man who worked with silver. He and his partners made statues that people worshipped in the temple. I told the people about the real God. I explained that God was real, not a man-made statue. Some people believed in Jesus and stopped buying the statues. The men were afraid that they might lose their business; they grabbed two of my friends and ran to a theater. The whole city followed them and began shouting. The shouting went on for two hours. Finally, the city clerk calmed the people down and told them to go home and my friends were not hurt. The men did not know or care that Jesus is life. They were spiritually dead. They did not know they needed to choose between life and death. Jesus defeated death and won the victory when He died on the cross and rose again. The person who trusts in Jesus' life in this world will have true life forever.

In another town, I was speaking to a room full of believers one evening. Around midnight, a young man sitting in the window went to sleep and fell three stories to the ground. He was dead. I ran outside, threw myself on him, put my arms around him, and said, "He's alive!" The believers knew that it was God's power that did this miracle, not mine. Then we all went back upstairs and talked until early morning.

Everywhere I went someone wanted to hurt me because of what I said about who Jesus was—especially in the city of Jerusalem. I told my friends that I must go to Jerusalem. The Holy Spirit impressed upon me that troubles and jail awaited me, but my life was not my concern. I wanted to complete my mission of telling people about Jesus.

The believers prayed for me, as I got ready to go. A prophet named Agabus borrowed my belt and used it to tie his hands and feet. He said, "The Holy Spirit says that the man who owns this belt will be tied up like this." The believers begged me not to go to Jerusalem. I told them I was ready to be tied up and to die for the Lord Jesus. Jesus was my life.

Our old life died with Jesus on the cross. We do not live in our own strength anymore—we have Christ's strength living in us. Of course, we still physically live in our body, but spiritually we live by faith in the Son of God. God gave us a new life in Jesus.

If you are a believer, will you trust Jesus to meet all of your needs and not put your trust in other people or things or money? If so, pray the following prayer to God:

Dear God, I am Your child, but I have been using people, achievements, and possessions to try to meet my needs. This is depending on myself instead of upon God. This doesn't satisfy me! Thank You that You meet all my needs. I want You to live through me. Thank You that You created me to be loved by You. I want to experience Your love and to let Your love flow out from me onto others.

Use Acts 19:23 to 21:14 and the Story to help you complete your Response. Then do the Activity.

1. Paul told people about the real God. He explained that God was real, not a man-made statue.

   ❑ True ❑ False

2. The men did not know or care that Jesus is __________________. They were spiritually ____________. They did not know they needed to choose between ____________________ and ____________________.

3. The person who trusts in Jesus' life in this world will have true life ________________________.
   a. forever
   b. temporarily

4. Paul wanted to complete his mission of telling ____________________________ about Jesus.

5. Paul told them he was ready to be tied up and to ____________________ for the Lord Jesus.
   a. die
   b. cry
   c. argue

6. Our old life ______________ with Jesus on the ________________. We do not live in our ____________________ anymore—we have Christ's strength living in us. Of course, we still physically live in our body, but spiritually we live by ________________ in the Son of God.

7. Read this verse: "But none of these things move me; nor do I count my life dear to myself" (Acts 20:24).

Now write a letter to God or draw a picture about when you knew you surrendered your life to God, if you have done this. If you have not done this, then write a letter to God or draw a picture about what you think surrendering your life to God would be like. Are you afraid He will ask you to do something you don't want to do? Or, do you think you might have to give up something you may not want to give up?

Young Children: Draw a picture of the people praying for Paul.

Christ Is Life

The cross is the only solution for surrendering our will; it represents brokenness. The purpose of brokenness is to highlight the fact that only God can meet our real needs. The times of greatest struggle and heartache can be the times of greatest spiritual discovery.

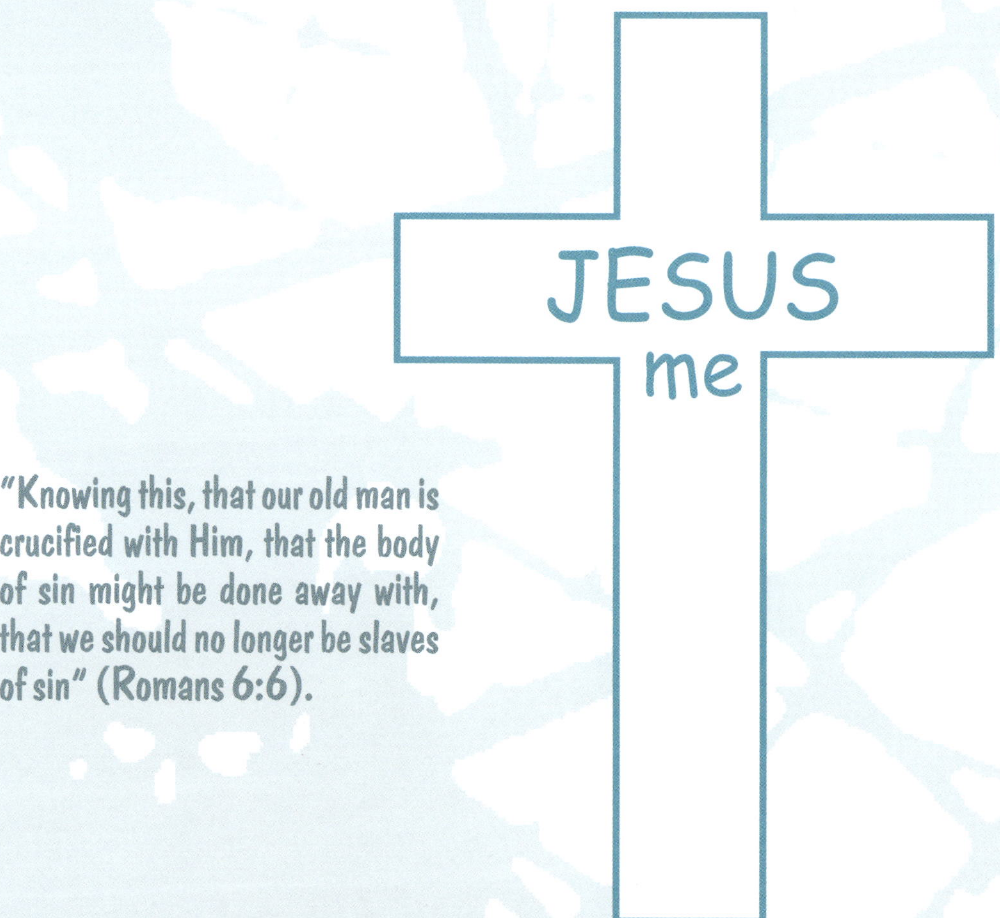

"Knowing this, that our old man is crucified with Him, that the body of sin might be done away with, that we should no longer be slaves of sin" (Romans 6:6).

What is life to you? Is it athletics? Being popular? Being beautiful? Rich? The world tells us these things are necessary for us to be happy, but they are not. They are substitutes for the real thing . . . Jesus' life that He gave for you.

Write the following things on the cross that apply to you and that you may have to surrender: Athletics, lots of friends, grades, good looks, personality, behavior (good or bad), or peer approval. Surrender these things to Jesus and you will experience real life.

Episode 30

Paul: Walking in the Light

How do we live in grace? Grace is the Lord Jesus living His life in and through us. It is no longer our life. He gave us His life in exchange for our old life of sin. What a deal! We do not have to measure up to any expectation. It is His life. He lives His life through us.

God has planned good works for us to walk in. This is impossible for us to do on our own, so we can relax and surrender our lives to God. He will impact other people's lives through us. What an awesome journey with God.

Now, use your imagination, as we journey back through time to look at the story, "Paul: Walking in the Light."

Story

(Story adapted from the New Testament books written by the Apostle Paul, the Gospels, and specifically Acts 21:15 to 26:32)

My name is Paul. As I traveled from city to city, telling people about Jesus, I saw how God's power can do more than I could ever have imagined.

I went to Jerusalem. I knew that the Jewish leaders would try to kill me for preaching about Jesus, but the Holy Spirit urged me to go. So I went. When I arrived, I met with the believers and went to the Temple. Seven days later, some of the Jews stirred up the crowd. They told lies about me and dragged me out of the Temple to kill me. The Roman commander came, and the people stopped beating me. But the commander arrested me. Then he asked who I was. The people in the crowd yelled different things, so the commander could not get the truth.

He let me speak to the people. I told them about my birthplace, my education, how I used to persecute the Christians, and about my experience on the road to Damascus. I told them that God told me to preach to non–Jews. At this, the crowd shouted, "Kill him!" The commander took me into the army building and prepared to beat me. I asked whether they had the right to do this to a Roman citizen. They immediately stopped and panicked because Roman citizens could not be put into chains or beaten without a trial. They almost got themselves in a heap of trouble! God is so good! He gave me the strength to endure this persecution. I didn't worry because He gave me the words to say.

The next morning, about 40 Jews decided that they would not eat or drink until they had killed me. My nephew found out and came and told me. I sent him to tell the commander, and he decided to take me to Governor Felix that night. Felix decided to hear my case. Five days later, the high priest, some of the older Jewish leaders, and a lawyer came before Felix and accused me of things they couldn't prove. They said I was a troublemaker. I told Felix that I was on trial for believing in the resurrection of the dead. Felix could not find me guilty of anything, but he left me in prison to please the Jews. Two years later, a man named Festus took over as governor. Again, the Jewish leaders brought charges against me. Again, I said I had done nothing against the Jewish law, the Temple, or Caesar. I wanted Caesar to hear my case.

While I waited to go to Rome, the Jewish King Agrippa and his sister Bernice came to visit Festus. They wanted to hear my case. I told King Agrippa my story, and that I prayed that he and all the people listening would believe in Jesus like I did. They left the room and discussed what to do about me. King Agrippa said, "He could have gone free, if he had not asked to go to Caesar."

God wanted me to go to Rome to preach about Jesus. He used my arrest and trials to give me an all–expense–paid trip, courtesy of the Roman government!

God's power in us can do more than we can imagine. God saved us and made us new people, so He could do through us the good works He planned for us. He wants to bring people into peace with Him. God will never stop working in you. As we depend upon Him and let Him work through us, He impacts other people's lives through us. Without Jesus, we can do nothing. But we can do all things through Him—He is our strength. There is no limit to what God can do.

Let's thank God that He has great plans for our lives. Pray these words of praise to Him:

God, as Your child, Your power in me can do more than I can imagine. Thank You that You will do through me the good works You have planned for me. You will never stop working in me. Without You, I can do nothing. There is no limit to what You can do.

Use Acts 21:15 to 26:32 and the Story to help you complete your Response. Then do the Activity.

1. Paul went to Jerusalem. The Jewish leaders encouraged him to preach about Jesus.

   ❑ True ❑ False

2. God told Paul to preach to _______________.

3. Paul didn't worry because _______________ gave him the words to say.
   a. Paul's nephew
   b. God
   c. the Roman commander

4. Paul told Felix that he was on trial for believing in ______________________________ ______________________________.

a. the resurrection of the dead
b. reincarnation
c. Caesar

5. God wanted Paul to go to Rome to preach about ________________. God will never stop ________________________ in you. Without Jesus, we can do ____________________________. There is __________ _____________ to what God can do.

6. Read this verse: "And Paul said, 'I would to God that not only you, but also all who hear me today, might become both almost and altogether such as I am, except for these chains'" (Acts 26:29).

Paul faced some really hard times after he chose to follow Jesus. No matter what he went through, Paul did not worry because he knew two things: Jesus loved him and Jesus had power over life and death. That meant Paul could be confident in Jesus, even when it looked like death was coming. Do you ever worry? As believers, part of having Christ inside us is freedom from worry. He is all powerful, even over death. Now write a letter to God or draw a picture about a time when you experienced freedom from worry, or about a time when you were very worried. Did your worrying have any effect on the situation?

Young Children: Draw a picture of Paul in jail.

Victory is a Person

As a Christian, do you have a loving heart? Yes. Do you always act like it? No. How can we experience victory?

The world views victory as something earned or worked for or achieved. How does God view victory? God views victory as a gift because victory is a Person. Jesus is our victory.

Does God have expectations for you? Are there things you need to do to stay holy or please Him? If so, what are they? Will reading the Bible, praying, going to church, being helpful to others and witnessing about Jesus make you holy? If so, how are you doing?

	1	2	3	4	5	6	7	8	9	10
reading the Bible										
praying										
going to church										
being helpful to others										
witnessing about Jesus										

Color the graph. Use a pen and lightly color in the graph according to how you are doing on the scale from 1 to 10. (1 = not doing well and 10 = doing extremely well.)

If you have a low score, you might feel shame, embarrassment, or like you want to withdraw. If you have a high score, you might feel proud. All of these emotions are performance-based responses.

God has a better way. He takes us off the treadmill of performance. He does not look at what we do in our own strength. He just wants us to live in His strength. We have a choice to make—live out of our own strength, or allow Christ to live through us. As we walk in His life our soul (mind, will, and emotions) begins to be transformed.

We can think about life like a race. There are many people on the sidelines, some cheering for you, encouraging you, and some are trying to trip you. If you fall (sin), just keep your eyes focused on Jesus and let Him love you. Then keep running in His strength. Remember – the victory has already been won! Jesus is standing at the finish line with His arms outstretched, waiting to hug you as you cross the finish line!

"But thanks be to God, who gives us the victory through our Lord Jesus Christ"
1 Corinthians 15:57.

Episode 31

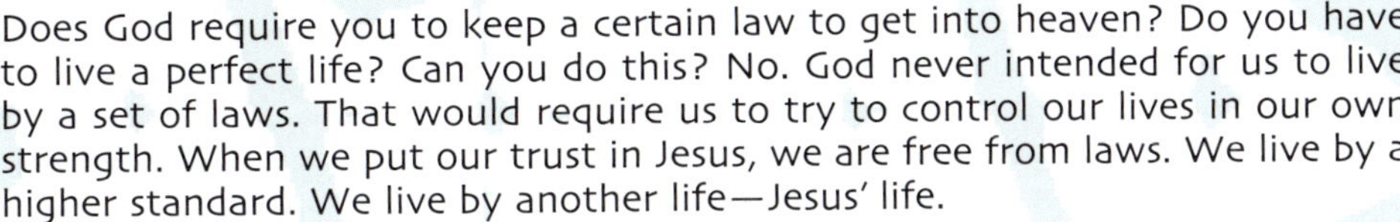

Paul: Relying on the Light

Does God require you to keep a certain law to get into heaven? Do you have to live a perfect life? Can you do this? No. God never intended for us to live by a set of laws. That would require us to try to control our lives in our own strength. When we put our trust in Jesus, we are free from laws. We live by a higher standard. We live by another life—Jesus' life.

Have you experienced Christ's life living in and through you? It's the only way to live a happy life. The Christian life is impossible to live, so let go of trying to live in your own strength and watch Jesus live His life through you. You'll be glad you did.

Now, use your imagination, as we journey back through time to look at the story, "Paul: Relying on the Light."

Story

(Story adapted from the New Testament books written by the Apostle Paul, the Gospels, and specifically Acts 27:1 to 28:31)

My name is Paul. In the last five episodes you've read about some of my adventures with God. You can read more about my life in the Bible—in the book of Acts or through the letters I wrote in the New Testament.

After my trial with Festus and King Agrippa, I set sail for Rome. The wind blew hard against us. I warned the sailors that we might lose the ship and our lives. Then a storm carried the ship off course. The sailors thought they would die. I informed them that the ship would be lost, but they would not die because God assured me that we would live. Some sailors wanted to abandon ship, but the ship's officer did not let them. The high winds continued and soon the big waves broke the ship to pieces. The soldiers wanted to kill the prisoners, so that none would swim away and escape, but the ship's officer said no to that idea. God was protecting me; He wanted me to live. The officer ordered everyone who could swim to jump into the water and swim to land. Everyone else used wooden planks and pieces of the ship to float to the shore.

The amazing thing was, I had freedom in Christ—even as a prisoner. Jesus frees us on the inside even when we are imprisoned by something in our circumstances. We don't have to follow laws to earn acceptance from God. Without Jesus, we can never be good enough for God. Only Jesus is perfect. So when He died on the cross to pay for our sins, God could make us perfect, holy, clean, and completely accepted.

When we arrived on the island, a snake bit me on the hand, but it didn't hurt me! The island people called me a god, but I told them it was the real God that protected my hand. Then, a leader on the island welcomed us into his home. I prayed for his sick father and God healed him too. After this, all the sick people on the island came to me, to be healed by God. After three months, we set sail for Rome. The island people supplied us with everything we needed for the journey. God turned a shipwreck into a blessing!

In Rome, I lived alone in a rented house. A guard stayed with me, since I was still under arrest. For two years, I preached about Jesus to everyone who visited me. No one tried to stop me.

I also wrote letters to the churches in other cities. Some of those letters are in the Bible. I wrote that Jesus said we had to be perfect just as God is perfect. That doesn't seem fair, does it? How can we perfectly love, forgive, and show kindness to others? The only way we can do any of this is to allow Christ to do it in and through us.

A person might follow all of God's laws, but if he fails to obey just one command, then the Bible says he is guilty of breaking the entire Law. We can try really hard to act good, but it is hopeless! No one is good enough—except Jesus, because He is perfect. We can stop trying so hard. Instead, know that He is God—not us. Saving and changing us is His work, not ours! He'll give you the faith to cooperate with Him, so He can carry out His good purposes in and through you.

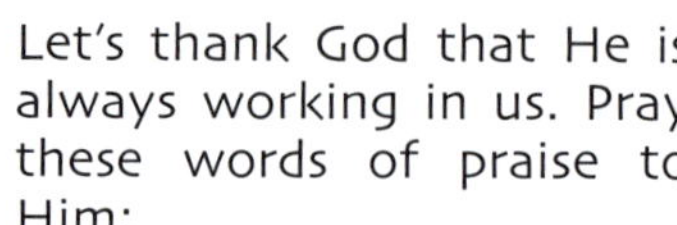

Let's thank God that He is always working in us. Pray these words of praise to Him:

God, thank You that I don't have to follow laws to earn acceptance from You. As a believer, You make me perfect, holy, clean and completely accepted. Thank You that I can stop trying so hard. You can carry out Your good purposes in and through me.

Use Acts 27:1 to 28:31 and the Story to help you complete your Response. Then do the Activity.

1. Paul warned the sailors that they might lose the ship but not their lives.

❑ True ❑ False

2. We don't have to follow ____________ to earn ______________________ from God. Only Jesus is perfect. So when He died on the cross to pay for our sins, God could make us __________________, __________, __________, and ____________________ ______________________.

3. We can try really hard to act good, but it is ____________________!

a. doable
b. admirable
c. hopeless

4. We can ____________ ________________ so hard. Instead, know that He is __________ —not us. Saving and changing us is _______ _________, not ours!

5. He'll give us the _______________ to cooperate with Him, so He can carry out His good purposes in and through us.

a. laws
b. faith
c. money

6. Read this verse: "[Paul was] preaching the kingdom of God and teaching the things which concern the Lord Jesus Christ with all confidence, no one forbidding him" (Acts 28:31).

What if there was a terrible disease in your neighborhood that killed everyone in its path. You had the only cure, and it was free and available to anyone who asked. They just had to know about it. What would you do? Would you share your good news or would you act afraid? The good news of Jesus is that He alone is life. Now write a letter to God or draw a picture about a time you felt confident in God and you allowed Christ to express His life through you.

Young Children: Draw a picture of the ship wreck and Paul making it to shore.

New Covenant

A covenant is like a contract. It says you do this and I'll do that. God made a holy contract with the Israelites. He said, "If you will be My people and obey Me, then I will be your God and protect and provide for you."

The Israelites kept breaking their end of the bargain (disobedience). When Jesus came to earth and died for us, He offered us a New Covenant. The New Covenant says "Jesus did it all (obeyed perfectly) and made a way for you to give up on the old selfish life and enter into new life."

In our new identity with Christ, we can experience peace, joy, and happiness on the inside no matter what else is happening around us.

To discover the Bible verse, unscramble the letters and place them in the spaces. (Use the chart below.)

A __ __ W __ K __ __ W T __ A T ALL T __ __ __ G __
L J A Y Q T J R Y W E L W L M M W E Z J B V

W __ __ K T __ G __ T __ __ __ __ __ __ G __ __ __ T __
Y R H T W R B Q W E Q H X R H B R R A W R

T __ O __ __ W __ __ L __ V __ G __ __. Romans 8:28
W E R V Q Y E R M R O Q B R A

A	B	C	D	E	F	G	H	I	J	K	L	M	N	O	P	Q	R	S	T	U	V	W	X	Y	Z
L	D	N	A	Q	X	B	E	Z	G	T	M	K	J	R	S	U	H	V	W	P	O	Y	I	F	C

Episode 1 - The Adventure Begins: Ultimate Friendship
1. True
2. (a) man and woman
3. life
4. Life Giver
5. Knowing that I am special to God and His most precious creation helps my family life, friendships, and activities. I experience His peace as I live life.
6. Example: God, You created me to think, feel, choose and imagine. Thank You that I am special to You as Your most precious creation.

Activity: 3, 5, 6, 1, 7, 4, 2
I learned that God cares for me. He wants good for me.

Episode 2 - Adam: Hiding from Love
1. The serpent lied to Eve because he is an enemy of God.
2. Adam and Eve were ashamed and afraid.
3. God knows where we are. He knows everything about us.
4. (a) to depend upon ourselves instead of upon God
5. True
6. They became like God, knowing good and evil . . . God wanted to protect them from eating the fruit from the tree of life and living forever.
7. (c) God is loving. He did not want Adam and Eve to have sin in them forever.
8. (c) loves us
9. Example: Dear God, I tried to hide from You when I got mad at my friend, and I felt ashamed about this. Thank You that You know everything about me. Thank You that You love me.

Activity: Words circled in the puzzle.

Episode 3 - Noah: Promise Made
1. (a) God felt pain in His heart because sin meant death for all people.
2. True
3. (b) Noah depended upon God. He built the ark before the rain started falling.
4. (c) God always keeps His promises.
5. Example: Dear God, my friend said she would come over for a visit, but she didn't show up. I felt abandoned, like she didn't care about me. But, I know You will never abandon me. You always care for me. I have done the same thing. I told my friend I would visit her, and I forgot. I felt terrible, and I didn't want that to happen again. I know You work all things for Your good. Thank You that You always keep Your promises.

Activity: Write God's promises on the rainbows. Make more rainbows with God's promises written on them, and give them to a friend.

Episode 4 - Abraham: Promise Kept
1. True
2. (a) Abraham listened to Sarah, and Ishmael was born.
3. (c) laughed
4. promise
5. Example: God, I didn't think You would ever bring me friends, but You gave me some great friends.

Activity: "Is anything too hard for the LORD?" (Genesis 18:14). No.

Episode 5 - Abraham: All About Faith
1. False – surprise; True – pride and joy
2. (b) knew God could be trusted
3. (c) "God will provide the lamb, my son."
4. (a) Isaac knew he could trust his father because his father depended upon God.
5. (c) God wanted Abraham to depend upon Him.
6. Example: I agreed to play a certain part in a school play not realizing I was supposed to be out of town with my family during the weekend of the play. It would be impossible for me to be in both places at the same time, so I needed a substitute. My friend, who is experienced in drama, volunteered to take my place in the play.

Activity: Abraham said, "My son, God will provide the lamb for a burnt offering."

Episode 6 - Jacob: From Deceit to Brokenness
1. True
2. (b) stew
3. Jacob, Esau
4. tricked
5. trusting, afraid
6. deceive, troubles
7. Example: My sister wanted to eat the last cookie, but I acted like I had already eaten it. When she wasn't looking, I quickly stuffed the last cookie into my mouth. Just then, she asked me a question and my mouth was full. She realized I had eaten the cookie after she asked me for it. I learned there is a good chance you might get caught if you are trying to deceive someone. I admitted what I had done, and my sister forgave me. I bought her a whole bag of cookies to show how much I appreciated her forgiveness! God gave me the grace to admit I was wrong and my sister the grace to forgive me.

Activity: Jealous, Hate, Anger, Bitter, Guilt, Shame

Episode 7 - Joseph: Bigger Than Our Troubles
1. True
2. Joseph's brothers threw him into a dry well. Then they sold him to some traders traveling to Egypt.
3. his house and everything he owned
4. the prisoners
5. Egypt to gather and store food during the seven years of plenty
6. Joseph could have been bitter and not served Potiphar well. If he had been bitter in prison, he may not have told the meanings of the dreams. That would have

prevented him from seeing Pharaoh. Or, Joseph may have worked extra hard for Potiphar and done any number of things to attempt to get out of going to prison. He might have boasted before Pharaoh and missed an opportunity to be taken out of prison and promoted. I hope I would have responded like Joseph, but I may have responded out of anger and frustration unless God intervened.
7. Example: God, only You could have allowed me to pass that test in school when I was failing. The teacher showed kindness by giving me extra help after school.

Activity: Example . . . my parents were never home when I needed them; someone said mean things about me; my coach yelled at me, so I felt pressure to perform for him. No.

Episode 8 - Joseph: Something Good
1. (a) bow down to him
2. Joseph's brothers bowed down to Joseph.
3. Joseph wanted to see if their heart attitudes had changed.
4. Potiphar put Joseph in charge of his house.
5. The prison warden put Joseph in charge of the prisoners. God showed Joseph what the king's servants' dreams meant.
6. Example: God, when my friend hurt me, You allowed us to talk about it, and we became closer friends.

Activity: Example . . . taken to the ball game after my dad wrongly disciplined me for something my other sibling did; ran into a friend when I was lost; opportunities came to me as a result of being sick; understood God's love more through the death of my pet; believed God more when I saw Him rescue my sibling from danger in the street; living more joyfully after experiencing pain in a relationship; experiencing God more through difficulties that drove me to read His Word; saved from injury when someone "jokingly" tried to hit me with a ball.

Episode 9 - Moses: His Power, Not Mine
1. False – seven people; True – seventy people
2. Moses saw an Egyptian man beating an Israelite man—one of his people. Moses killed the Egyptian. No. Moses tried to break up a fight between two Israelites, but they didn't want his help.
3. Moses was worried that the Israelites might not believe that God had appeared to him. He never could speak well. He begged God to send someone else.
4. (c) trust Him
5. (d) All of the above
6. God's power, not Moses' power, would bring the people out of Egypt.
7. Example: Someone asked me to sing a solo. I didn't think I could do it. I felt inadequate. But God could do it through me. God, thank You for Your power. Thank You that You are always with me.

Activity: I am the Lord. You can trust Me.

Episode 10 - Moses: Rescued
1. True
2. They didn't want to be rescued—not if it meant extra suffering!
3. ten
4. passed over
5. in control
God split the Red Sea, and the Israelites walked across on dry land. The Egyptian army chased them, but God made the waters come over the Egyptian army, and they all drowned.
6. Example: I cried because I was suffering emotionally when someone picked on me. Yes, God hears me when I cry. Yes, God is concerned about me. I need God to rescue me from their words. God, let me get my worth and value from what You say about me rather than what other people might say about me.

Activity: Pillar of cloud maze: to lead the way; Pillar of fire maze: to give them light

Episode 11 - Moses: Dependent
1. (a) They forgot how God had taken care of them in the past.
(b) They didn't believe that God had good plans for them.
(c) They wanted to be in control. They didn't understand that God was in control—and that He would take good care of them.
(d) While they were slaves, they had plenty of food. They thought that God had brought them out to the desert to die.
(e) They were afraid that God had forgotten about food!
2. God sent bread from the sky and flocks of quail (a kind of bird). God wanted them to rest on the seventh day, just like He did after creating the world. The food didn't rot on the seventh day.
3. measure up
4. God wanted them to depend upon Him instead of upon themselves.
5. Example: I was alone in my house when I suddenly felt afraid. I was afraid until I heard my friend in another part of the house. I didn't realize she was at my house. When I knew she was there, my fear went away.

Activity: I realize that I can't keep the Ten Commandments perfectly.

Episode 12 - Joshua: Courageous Trust
1. True
2. (b) red rope
3. power, protection
4. (b) strange orders
5. love, hearts
6. Example: I was walking down my street one night, and suddenly I felt afraid. Two of the streetlights were out, and I couldn't see what was in front of me. I felt all alone. But then I remembered that God was with me. He promised to always be with me. I just started talking to God. The fear disappeared, and I sensed His peace.

Activity: Joshua trusted God, even when it didn't make sense.

Episode 13 - Samson: It's Never Too Late
1. True
2. bare hands, Spirit of the Lord
3. strength, hair
4. (b) strength
5. Example: Dear God, I had to tell my friend I was sorry for using her computer without asking her. I was afraid I might lose my friendship. I was embarrassed to tell her. I didn't think I could do it. Then she mentioned that I was free to use her computer anytime I wanted. This gave me an easy way to tell her what I had already done. She was okay with this. I believe God worked in me, and this strengthened our friendship.

Activity: Nazirite, Samson's strength was in his hair.

Episode 14 - Ruth: A New Life
1. True
2. (b) accepted
3. Boaz told Ruth to stay in his field, gather grain, and get water when she was thirsty. He invited her to come and eat with him.
4. Boaz bought back the land.
5. new life
6. Example: Dear Mom and Dad, thank you for wanting me and accepting me. Thank you for making me a part of your family. You take care of me by providing food, shelter, and clothing. Thank you for these things. Thank you for the new life you give me.

Activity:
1. adopts
2. restores
3. redeem
4. foreigner
5. family
6. grace

Adoption Certificate
[your name] is a (4) foreigner. Joshua has shown (6) grace to [your name]. Joshua chooses to (3) redeem [your name] and his/her family's property. Joshua accepts [your name] and promises to give [your name] everything he/she needs. On this day, Joshua (2) restores and (1) adopts [your name]. [your name] is now part of Joshua's (5) family.

Episode 15 - David: Conquering Our Giants
1. True
2. loved, depended upon
3. (b) hearts
4. one
5. (a) nine
6. fear
7. Lord of heaven's armies
8. (c) ran
9. Example: Dear God, I saw a man roaming in the streets. I thought he was a "bum," but I later found out he helped street people. I got to know him and he was a great man with a big heart.

Activity: Find the words in the puzzle

Episode 16 - David: Day of Discovery
1. False – delighted; True – made King Saul jealous
2. (c) kill
3. best friend
4. (b) gave up his right
5. confession, consequences
6. an intimate personal relationship with God
7. King of all kings and the Lord of all lords!
8. Example: God, when my grandmother died I wanted to know about Your eternal kingdom. I wanted to know if I might see her again. You assured me that there is a place reserved for your children.

Activity: David waited on God's timing to become Israel's king.

Episode 17 - Esther: Trusting God for the Moment at Hand
1. False – came with them; True – refused to come
2. Queen Esther
3. one true God
4. (c) killed
5. risk her life
6. Example: My basketball coach was drawing up a play for the last shot of the game, but I thought we should try something different. I took a risk and told him my idea, even though he could have made me sit on the bench for that. He decided to use my strategy, and we won the game. I felt this was a way that God showed my coach, the other players, and me the value of each individual. When we trust God, He can use each of us in amazing ways for the greater good of everyone.

Activity: Mordecai, King Xerxes, Esther, Mordecai, Haman, Haman, Esther

Episode 18 - Job: Unanswered "Why's"
1. False – weakest; True – strongest
2. motives
3. Who He was, gave him
4. (b) falsely accused
5. trust Him
6. last, first
7. Example: My grandpa was so sick he had to go to the hospital. I didn't understand why God would let that happen because he had walked with God for so many years. Then I found out that while he was there, my grandpa had the chance to talk to several doctors and nurses about God's love. He told them about his personal relationship with God through Jesus. I realized that God can even use sickness to get the "Good News" to people.

Activity: Example . . . God is all–knowing: He knows everything

Episode 19 - Daniel: Experiencing God in Hard Times
1. False – celebrated with; True – destroyed
2. (b) "God is the God of gods, the Lord of kings, and a revealer of secrets."
3. one, true, God
4. close the mouths of the lions

5. God is always there
6. Example: Picture of Shadrach, Meshach, and Abed–Nego in the fiery furnace with God protecting them.

Activity: Male lions can live up to 12 years in the wild. Female lions can live up to 18 years. The male lion has the beautiful mane. Picture drawn of Daniel in the lion's den.

Episode 20 - Jonah: No More Running
1. False – good hearts; True – evil
2. running away
3. believed in
4. True
5. Promised One
6. (b) cares for
7. Example: God, I was hurting when my friend sent a picture of me to some people that I didn't want to have the picture. I surrendered my right to keep that picture private from the other people, and I experienced Your peace.

Activity: The correct order . . . ran away, ship, storm, overboard, swallowed by fish, went to Nineveh, preached to the people, new life

Episode 21 - John the Baptist: Preparing the Way
1. True
2. God's gift
3. prophet of God
4. (c) the Lord
5. greater, Son of God
6. Example: My friend and I have always been competitive—in school, in sports, in everything we do. Recently, I've been learning that it's OK to compete, but what's more important is to help others be the best they can be—even if it helps them be better than me. If my only focus is to win, I can act prideful, and God hates an arrogant attitude. But when I think of others first, it demonstrates a humble attitude—an attitude that is expressed by Christ in my heart.

Activity: others, prideful, first, all, God, attitude

Episode 22 - Mary: Mother of Jesus
1. True
2. (c) box where animals are fed
3. (b) an angel of the Lord
5. Promised One, takes away
6. Example: Picture of my favorite part of the Christmas story, the night Jesus was born in a manger.

Activity: Unscrambled words . . . angels, star, Promised one, Mary, shepherds, Joseph, wise men, Jesus

Episode 23 - Jesus Christ: My Friend
1. Sin
2. True
3. measures up
4. death
5. (b) took the blame for everyone's sins—past, present, and future. (c) took on the payment—death—for everyone's sins.
6. people could live forever with God and experience His joy
7. Salvation. No, it's a free gift.
8. (e) All of the above
9. Example: Dear God, thank You that Jesus died for my sins. He gave me His life. Thank You that You adopted me as Your child. Yes. [or] No. Date

Activity: "Jesus said . . . 'I am the way, the truth, and the life. No one comes to the Father except through Me'" (John 14:6). Jesus, Jesus

Episode 24 - Peter: Peer Pressure
1. True
2. (b) a rooster crowed
3. (c) die
4. (a) Jesus
5. serve others
6. trust
7. forgiven, courage
8. Example: I openly declared my faith in Jesus until the eighth grade, when I invited one of my soccer teammates to go to church with me. He immediately nicknamed me "preacher boy." For weeks, I avoided talking about my faith. But finally, I realized that I could trust Jesus to enable me with the courage to say what He wanted to say through me to my soccer team. I didn't know how I would be treated, but I did know that I could trust Jesus—no matter what happened.

Activity: rooster, impulsive, cried, jumped, forgiven, sheep, living proof

Episode 25 - Peter: Learn from Failure
1. True
2. silver or gold, better
3. (c) Jesus
4. God, men
5. True
6. Jesus, saved
7. Example: My friend, Josh, was in a car accident, and he had to sit in a wheelchair. He used to play ball with us at recess, but after that most of the kids just ignored him. I know that made him feel bad because he was still the same person. The Bible says that God loves and accepts all people. Because I'm a child of God, I can trust Him to enable me to accept all people too—even when they are different from me. Every day I enjoyed spending time with Josh, and he didn't feel all alone.

Activity: Jesus accepts all people, just the way they are.

Episode 26 - Paul: Light from Heaven
1. True
2. (b) light
3. Jesus
4. God's Son
5. (c) love letter
6. (c) all

7. Example: Dear God, thank You for saving me from sin and from myself. You pursued me and revealed Yourself to me. That's the most special thing You could have ever done—giving me Your life, Your eternal life. I'm in awe of You. Thank You that You live Your forever life in me. You teach me so many intimate secrets. It's amazing how You love my parents, my friends, and even my enemies through me.

Activity: Words from Acts 9:3 and Romans 5:8–10 circled in the puzzle.

Episode 27 - Paul: Receiving the Light
1. True
2. evil
3. non–Jews
4. (c) human beings
5. religious laws
6. the Holy Spirit, clay jars
7. Example: Dear God, I went through troubles when I had an argument with my best friend. I was crying all alone in my room, but You were there with me living Your life in me. Thank You for never leaving me.

Activity: Joy, patience, gentleness, peace, kindness, self–control, and purity are in the "Jesus" column. Idolatry, witchcraft, envy, drunkenness, hate and troublemaking are in the "Flesh" column.

Episode 28 - Paul: Reflecting the Light
1. False – helping; True – calling out to them
2. shaking with fear, saved
3. (c) his true identity as a child of God with all of Christ's power inside of him
4. worshipped
5. (b) Jesus
6. old life, new life, God's family, one, union
7. Yes, it was amazing. Example: Dear God, You worked through my life to encourage my friend when he was going through a relationship trial. You allowed Your joy in suffering and comfort to be expressed through me. It is great to participate with what You are doing.

Activity: Water is poured into the cup and stirred together with the drink powder mix. Holy, righteous, and valuable and accepted are written on the cup.

Episode 29 - Paul: Trusting the Light
1. True
2. life, dead, life, death
3. (a) forever
4. people
5. (a) die
6. died, cross, own strength, faith
7. Example: Dear God, there is such freedom knowing that I have surrendered my life to you. You revealed to me that my life wasn't my life anymore, but I had been bought with a price. The price was the blood of Your Son, Jesus. The great news is that after death comes resurrection. Thank You that I am resurrected with Christ.

Activity: Athletics, lots of friends, grades, good looks, personality, behavior (good or bad), or peer approval are written on the cross.

Episode 30 - Paul: Walking in the Light
1. False – encourage; True – try to kill
2. non–Jews
3. (b) God
4. (a) the resurrection of the dead
5. Jesus, working, nothing, no limit
6. Sometimes. Example: Dear God, I believe You spoke through me when I shared a story about You with a friend. You were powerful through me. I didn't worry about what I was saying because I knew You were speaking through me.

Activity: The graph is colored according to how one is doing on the scale from one to ten.

Episode 31 - Paul: Relying on the Light
1. False – not their lives; True – and their lives
2. laws, acceptance, perfect, holy, clean, and completely accepted
3. (c) hopeless
4. stop trying, God, His work
5. (b) faith
6. I would tell everyone I saw. I would go out into the streets and tell everyone. I wouldn't act afraid. Example: Dear God, I felt so confident in You that when I visited my relative I allowed You to express yourself through me with a few words of encouragement and a few loving hugs. You are amazing.

Activity: The letters are unscrambled and put in the spaces to discover the Bible verse. "And we know that all things work together for good to those who love God" Romans 8:28.